CHRISTMAS

WITH

Victoria™

1998

CHRISTMAS
WITH
Victoria
1998

Oxmoor
House®

HEARST COMMUNICATIONS, INC.

Christmas with _Victoria_ ™ 1998

©1998 Hearst Communications, Inc., and
Oxmoor House, Inc.

Victoria is a trademark of Hearst Communications, Inc.
Oxmoor House, Inc.
Book Division of Southern Progress Corporation
P.O. Box 2463, Birmingham, AL 35201

Library of Congress Catalog Card Number: 98-65704
ISBN: 0-8487-1846-1
ISSN: 1093-7633
Manufactured in the United States of America
First Printing 1998

We're here for you!
We at Oxmoor House are dedicated to serving you with reliable information that expands your imagination and enriches your life. We welcome your comments and suggestions. Please write us at:

> Oxmoor House, Inc.
> **Editor, Christmas with _Victoria_**
> 2100 Lakeshore Drive
> Birmingham, AL 35209

To order additional publications, call (205) 877-6560.

Victoria

Editor-in-Chief: Nancy Lindemeyer
Editorial Director: Deborah Beaulieu
Art Director: Susan Maher
Executive Editor: Mary Aurea Morris
Market Editor: Susan George
Photography/Finance Editor: Marie-Lucie Charlot
Contributing Editor: Nicole Esposito
Field Editor: Ann Levine

Oxmoor House, Inc.

Editor-in-Chief: Nancy Fitzpatrick Wyatt
Senior Homes Editor: Mary Kay Culpepper
Senior Foods Editor: Susan Payne Stabler
Senior Editor, Editorial Services: Olivia Kindig Wells
Art Director: James Boone

Christmas with _Victoria_ 1998

Editor: Adrienne S. Davis
Foods Editor: Janice Krahn Hanby
Associate Art Director: Cynthia R. Cooper
Designer: Rita A. Yerby
Copy Editors: L. Amanda Owens, Catherine S. Ritter,
    Donna Baldone
Editorial Assistant: Kaye Howard Smith
Writer: Virginia Gilbert Loftin
Senior Photographer: Jim Bathie
Photographer: Brit Huckabay
Senior Photo Stylist: Kay E. Clarke
Assistant Photo Stylist: Jan Gautro
Illustrators: Kelly Davis, Anita S. Bice
Publishing Systems Administrator: Rick Tucker
Director, Production and Distribution: Phillip Lee
Associate Production Manager: Vanessa C. Richardson
Production Assistant: Faye Porter Bonner

Contents

Foreword

We are pleased to bring you **Christmas with** *Victoria* **1998,** *a collection of ideas for decorations, gifts, menus, and more. You'll draw inspiration from the beautiful color photographs, luscious recipes, and creative ideas featured on these pages.* **Christmas with** *Victoria* **1998** *is your guide to creating a meaningful and memorable holiday.*

Whether you choose to celebrate this season simply or at the height of formality, **Christmas with** *Victoria* **1998** *suggests creative new ways to open your doors to friends and family, sharing the warmth and spirit of the holidays. We wish you a holiday that will linger in memory—a season filled with laughter, quiet reflection, and the company of loved ones.*

From the **Victoria** *family, a merry Christmas to you and to all who share this holiday in your home—and in your heart.*

Editors of **Christmas with** *Victoria*

Chapter I

Decorations

Trim the tree until it glitters, swag the mantel with greenery, and fill the house with the unmistakable color and fragrance of your favorite flowers.

Gather together a musical collection, including a violin, penny whistle, a pair of sleigh bells, sheet music of a beloved carol, and a set of brass handbells, to nestle beside the Christmas tree.

Grace a mantel with a simple arrangement of flowers and greenery in a lovely footed bowl. Add a few votive candles for a holiday glow.

Favorite Things

Dress your house for Christmas with a combination of everyday and holiday treasures.

Because the accessories in your home infuse the rooms with your spirit, there is no need to put them away at Christmastime. Use them instead to make a grand holiday statement by displaying them in unexpected ways.

Gather your finest bowls and vases—sterling, crystal, or porcelain—and fill them with beautiful blooms. Layer fine linens on the sideboard or hall table, perhaps tying them in stacks with lengths of pretty ribbon for a holiday accent. Group candlesticks of varying heights for a dramatic tabletop effect.

Assemble a collection of silver serving pieces for a shining centerpiece or set them on the mantel atop a bed of greens.

Embellish framed family photographs with greenery and flowers. Tie lengths of moiré or organdy ribbon around sofa pillows or stacks of books, choosing a color that harmonizes with the tones you use everyday. Red and green are the traditional colors of Christmas, but if they clash with your room, use ivory, ecru, white, royal blue, gold, or silver for a pleasing combination.

Lilies, golden rope, and tiny musical instruments dress the mantel clock for an elegant evening.

The simplest decoration of all is also the most natural—sprigs of holly and berries in the snow.

Holly Days

Each glossy sprig recalls the colors of Christmas.

The ancient Chinese used holly to decorate for their New Year's celebrations. Romans chose it to symbolize Saturnalia, the midwinter feast, exchanging boughs as tokens of friendship and good will; they also thought it a charm to ward off evil and lightning. In Old England, holly was said to provide a safe haven for fairies and elves. To Native Americans, it signified courage and eternal life.

Even without such legends, holly's brilliant red berries and evergreen leaves seem custom-made for Christmas. Once cut, holly retains its shape and color for several days, making it a durable choice for outdoor decorations. Holly will not last as long in drier climates or indoors and should be kept moist with a daily spritz of water.

Most holly plants are easy to grow, and some will literally live for centuries. (An American holly reportedly planted by George Washington still thrives at Mount Vernon.) Most evergreen varieties require companionship: a female tree for berries and a male planted 30 yards away to ensure pollination. An American holly grows to 40 or 50 feet in mass, but a Foster holly, a hybrid of American and Dahoon, usually reaches no more than 25 feet. A fast-growing Savannah holly produces similar growth to that of a Foster but with lovely oval leaves without spikes or sharp spines.

Careful pruning enhances the berry yield. First, remove lateral branches that grow inward and then remove a fourth to a third of all berried sprays to encourage branching. Leave lower limbs with inferior sprays to suppress weed growth.

Have a bucket of water ready to receive the harvest of sprays and try to keep the branches out of direct sunlight and wind to protect the berries. Handle them with care to prevent damaging berries or scratching leaves, which will cause discoloration.

Make swags and wreaths from holly alone or combine it with other evergreens, such as pine, boxwood, fir, and juniper, for texture and fragrance. Variegated leaves and yellow or orange berries add visual interest to holiday decorations.

A wreath of holly is a long-lived outdoor decoration.

Holly and Berry Wreath

Wear thick gloves to protect your hands from the sharp points of the holly leaves as you craft a lush wreath.

You will need: Clippings from a variety of holly plants; florist's picks with wire; 20"-diameter straw wreath form; thick gloves; florist's wire; and ribbon to trim.

1. Gather 3 to 4 sprigs of holly, pinching the stems together to hold the clippings in place. Secure the holly bunch to the florist's pick by wrapping the wire on the pick tightly around the stems and pick. Be sure the pointed end of the florist's pick is facing away from the greenery.

2. Insert the pointed end of the florist's pick and stems into the straw wreath form, securing the holly bunch to the wreath form. Repeat steps 1 and 2 to cover the front and sides of the wreath form with holly bunches. Leave the back of the wreath form uncovered so it hangs flat against a door or wall.

3. For a hanger, cut a 6" piece of florist's wire. Thread 1 end of the wire through the form, stringing the form onto the wire piece. Form the wire into a loop by twisting the ends of the wire tightly together.

4. Trim the wreath with ribbon as desired. For this wreath, we looped the ribbon around the wreath, moving the ribbon from the inside of the wreath to the outside.

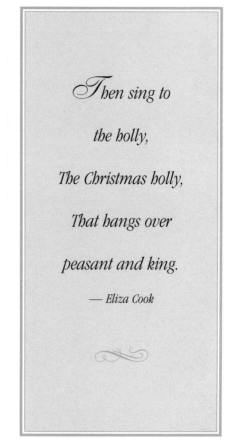

Then sing to

the holly,

The Christmas holly,

That hangs over

peasant and king.

— Eliza Cook

Hand-painted with enamel, this beautiful ornament bears holly-and-berry clusters.

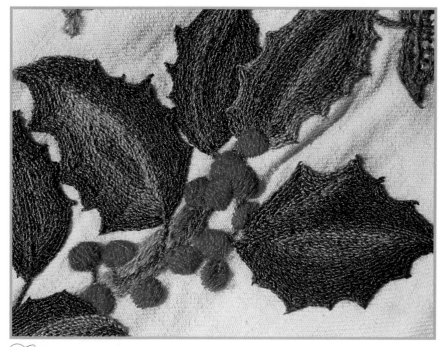

Crewel wool is stitched onto Belgian linen in a familiar holiday symbol, reminiscent of seventeenth-century Jacobean tapestry.

A humble basket is pressed into service. It holds a ruff of evergreens, a few sprays of pepper berries, and deep red pomegranates sprinkled with a few drops of cinnamon essential oil.

Seasonal Scents

Experiment with herbs and spices to herald the season in fragrance.

Piney rosemary, aromatic cinnamon, spicy cloves, and sweet lavender—in nearly any combination, herbs and spices marry well to create enticing seasonal scents. Heap fresh rosemary, thyme, sage, and dried roses on a platter with bundles of dried orange slices tied with raffia. Or tuck tiny bunches of bay or lavender in a bowl of fruit and fill a basket with pomegranates, pepper berries, and juniper.

Whether you concoct a traditional or nontraditional potpourri, be sure to mix the ingredients well with a teaspoon or two of essential oil, perhaps mint, cinnamon, or orange. Place the mixture in a large plastic bag and add a tablespoon of fixative, such as orrisroot, then shake well. Let the mixture mature for a week or two, turning occasionally. This homemade potpourri will not smell as strong as commercial preparations; instead, it produces a pleasantly subtle scent.

Mix greenery, such as rosemary, thyme, sage, and juniper, with dried roses, tallow berries, and pepper berries. Blend four parts rose oil to one part cinnamon oil to enhance the spicy-sweet fragrance.

Christmas Potpourri

Prepare this sugar-and-spice scent several weeks ahead of time to allow it to mellow and set.

You will need: Crab or lady apples; whole cloves; 4 cups rosebuds and petals; 1 cup 1" cinnamon pieces; 3 or 4 salal (lemon) leaves; 3 or 4 tallow berry sprigs; 2 cedar rose or other tree cones; rose essential oil; cinnamon essential oil; bergamot essential oil; ½ cup oak moss; and several large dried roses for decoration.

1. Pierce each apple with cloves to make a small pomander. Mix the rosebuds, cinnamon pieces, leaves, tallow berries, cones, and mini pomanders together in a bowl.

2. In a separate bowl, stir the essential oils with the oak moss. Add this fragrant moss to the rosebud mixture. For essential oils, see Resources on page 140.

3. Pack the potpourri in a tightly sealed container. Place the container in a cool, dark place. Allow the potpourri to mellow in the container for several weeks, shaking the container occasionally.

4. When you are ready to use the potpourri, pour the mixture into a decorative bowl, making sure the berries, pomanders, and cones are on top of the mixture. Decorate the potpourri with large dried roses.

Make your garland long and full for a graceful cascade across and down the sides of the mantel.

Graceful Garland

A luxurious draping of fresh greens and flowers trims the mantel with cheer.

Whether stately or simple, formal or homey, the mantel offers a warming focal point for friends and family to gather during the holidays. Drape it with swags of rich velvet or brocade, add a grouping of favorite plates or vases, or gather your prettiest candlesticks in a pleasing arrangement.

A garland crafted from thick boughs of fresh Fraser fir creates a sumptuous and fragrant decoration that can be embellished to suit your whim. Handcrafted wire-mesh cones filled with bright flowers and fruits in holiday colors are a new rendition of a traditional cornucopia. For the cones, see Resources on page 140.

Garden Cornucopias

Glorious flower- and fruit-filled cones nestle amid boughs of Fraser fir.

You will need (for 1 cornucopia): 1 florist's foam brick; desired cone-shaped container or basket; small plastic bag; sheet moss; flowers, such as fresh red and white roses; fruits, such as kumquats, lady apples, and Seckel pears; sprigs of greenery, such as cedar, holly, and nandina; florist's picks; and florist's wire.

1. Cut a piece of florist's foam to fit inside the cone. Soak the foam piece in water until it is saturated. To prevent water from leaking, place the foam inside a small plastic bag, leaving the top of the foam uncovered.

2. Line the inside of the cone with small pieces of moss, leaving space at the opening of the cone for the foam. Tuck the plastic-wrapped foam into the moss inside the cone opening.

3. Fill the cone as desired with flowers, fruits, and greenery. Strip the leaves from the flowers and insert the stems into the foam. Insert the greenery stems into the foam as well. To secure the fruit in the cone, mount the fruit on a florist's pick. Break the florist's pick about 5" from its pointed end. Press the pointed end into the bottom of the fruit. Insert the broken end of the pick into the foam.

4. Nestle the filled cone within the garland or secure the cone to the garland with florist's wire.

Fill mesh cones with red and white roses, kumquats, and bright green pears, then accent with sprigs of pepper berries.

Fine organdy ribbon weaves in and out of the bouquet-filled cones placed at the garland's midpoint.

Ivory tapers illuminate an angel-topped basket holding satin pillows trimmed in ribbons.

Candles shaped and scented like pears are artfully placed on an oval mirror and twined with a starry garland.

Christmas by Candlelight

Let the warmth of candlelight fill each room, setting a tranquil mood for every celebration.

rom slender tapers to petite votives and every shape in between, candles claim a place in the holiday home, symbolizing peace and summoning remembrance.

Candlelight reflected in silver and crystal softens every silhouette in its cast. The inviting glow of a candelabra centerpiece draws friends and family together around the table.

Though specialty shops sell a profusion of scented, shaped, and colored candles, making your own is simple and satisfying—and using them, even more so.

There are two ways of spreading light: to be the candle or the mirror that reflects it.

— Edith Wharton

At the table's center, crystal bowls of water hold handmade candles and tallow berries.

Glowing Centerpieces

The holiday table shines with candles afloat in crystal compotes and bowls.

You will need: Empty, clean aluminum coffee can; 1 (16-ounce) package household paraffin; aluminum foil; metal pastry tins or candy molds; stiff wax-coated wicks fitted with metal wick tabs (available at crafts stores); large glass bowls or compotes; and desired greenery and flowers.

1. Place the coffee can in a pan of water on the stove over medium-low heat. Melt the paraffin in the coffee can.

2. Cover your work surface with aluminum foil. In the center of each pastry tin or candy mold, position a wick with the tab flat against the bottom of the tin or mold.

3. Using pot holders to hold the hot coffee can, carefully pour the melted paraffin into each tin or mold until the paraffin is about ⅛" from the top. If necessary, quickly adjust the wick.

4. Carefully place the filled tins or molds in a shallow pan filled with cold water. The water should be level with the wax.

5. The paraffin will harden in about an hour. Holding each candle by the wick, gently pull the paraffin from the tin or mold.

6. For a centerpiece, arrange the candles in a bowl or compote filled with enough water to float the candles about 1" from the top of the bowl. Float flowers and greens in the bowl among the candles.

Fresh roses combine with handmade candles to float gracefully in a bowl. Make sure the candle-and-flower arrangement is not too crowded.

Handmade angels and Santas decorate this grandly scaled tree, anchored in an old-fashioned tin tub.

Farmhouse Christmas

Simplicity is a reminder of Christmases past, when handmade decorations filled the house with comfort and joy.

A nineteenth-century Christmas was a study in the generosity of nature and ingenuity of clever hands. The spirit of a farmhouse Christmas can be recaptured, even in a city dwelling, with decorations fashioned from winter's spare beauty and placed amid more elegant accessories.

Wreaths made of vines and twigs are cheery and winter-hardy ornaments for outside doors and windows. They are especially eye-catching when trimmed with a dusting of snow or fringe of icicles.

Trim the tree with handcrafted ornaments made of scrap fabrics and hung from raffia. String garlands and fill baskets with all-natural Christmas ornaments such as fruits, nuts, bright red holly, or nandina berries.

A galvanized tin bucket can serve as a tree stand; steady the trunk with heavy stones or bricks hidden by a layer of large pinecones. Allow the tin container to show for a bit of homespun charm, or surround it with a patchwork quilt or tartan blanket.

On the following pages, branches of fir and cedar are used as natural garlands and swags to tuck behind a painting. Shiny glass ornaments fill an antique box instead of hanging on the tree. And brocade ribbon bows adorn candlesticks to add a touch of holiday cheer.

Ivy topiaries trained into hearts and globes are evergreen accents for the sideboard or table, and spheres of supple vines wound into kissing balls perch atop a stack of books.

A small tree, decorated with aromatic orange slices suspended with twine, stands on a tabletop. Treasured toys and an antique train are placed beneath the branches to remind all of happy times.

A vine wreath adds a simple flourish to the back of a porch rocker; a larger, fuller version graces the weathered door. Sleigh bells dangling from the doorknob signal the arrival of guests or the return of children just in time for cocoa and cookies.

Roses and pine soften a framed portrait and add a hint of fragrance. Gleaming glass balls peek from an antique box, candlesticks are tied with ribbon bows, and an antique pitcher blooms with a rose bouquet.

We hang everything on

our Christmas tree,

Ornaments big and bright,

and all of these

sparkling icicles

and twirling balls

of white.

— Kay Thompson

An antique lantern and sprigs of pine and berries gladden a side table. A heart-shaped ivy topiary such as this lasts beyond the holiday season.

Tiny lights glow through translucent slices of dried oranges suspended from twine on a tabletop tree.

On a tree dusted with snow, a blown-glass Father Christmas finds shelter beneath an antique glass bird.

A Touch of Glass

An old-world art becomes a prized part of Christmas present.

It seems fitting that Germany, where the custom of the Christmas tree originated, is also the birthplace of the glass Christmas ornament.

Glassblowers in the village of Lauscha, Germany, began making the first glass ornaments in the early nineteenth century. These large, hollow blown-glass balls were called *kugels.* Left smooth and shiny or decorated with hot wax for a textured finish, they were hung from ceilings and windows to ward off evil spirits.

By 1890 German glass ornaments were all the rage in America, thanks to five-and-dime merchant F. W. Woolworth, whose initial $25 order of the German exports eventually became a $25 million enterprise. Demand for the ornaments led to more fanciful shapes, such as pinecones, animals, birds, fish, fruits, and musical instruments, some of which actually made sounds.

Now highly valued by collectors, German hand-blown glass figural ornaments in pristine condition command prices up to several hundred dollars apiece. Father Christmas and Santa Claus ornaments are especially prized and may be found at antique stores, flea markets, and estate sales. However, common figural and post-war West German ornaments remain inexpensive because so many of them were produced.

Serious collectors warn novices to beware of reproductions sold as antiques and suggest a simple way to test for age: sniff the inside of the piece. If it is an antique, the inside gives off a musty smell.

Storing Ornaments

Pack your special or antique ornaments with care to keep them safe from year to year. Cartons designed for ornament storage are available in many stores, though sturdy boxes from the wine shop—complete with cardboard dividers—work just as well.

Wrap each ornament in several layers of white tissue paper, bubble wrap, or plain newsprint (do not use the daily newspaper, as the printer's ink may rub off on your treasures). Place the wrapped ornament on a bed of packing paper or plastic foam pieces, taking care not to overpack the box. Fill around the ornaments with additional packing materials so the ornaments do not move about inside the box.

Label the contents of the box and store it at room temperature, not in the attic or cellar, where temperatures and humidity can fluctuate dramatically during the year.

Mound glass fruit ornaments with fresh greenery in a footed crystal bowl for a festive centerpiece (right). Each plate bears a sprig of greenery tied with a velvet bow and adorned with a glass bird and pear (above). The redbird is flocked with glitter and boasts a spun-glass tail. The pear has a glistening, granulated texture.

Family photos become holiday keepsakes when framed with ribbon mats.

Wrapped in Ribbon

A spiraling strand, a festive bow—the right ribbon adds a touch of pure magic.

A beautiful length of ribbon lends luxury to holiday decorating. Silk, satin, or velvet—striped, plaid, or solid—the choice is yours. And in your hands the possibilities are limited only by your imagination.

Narrow ribbons are handy for hanging ornaments on the tree; slightly wider ribbons are suitable for tying around the base of candlesticks. Wire-edged ribbon, sold in crafts and specialty shops, is easy to shape into lasting folds. Available in luxurious fabrics as well as humble cotton, nubby burlap, and materials designed for outdoor use, wire-edged ribbon has thin strands of flexible wire along both edges, allowing even a novice to create festive bows.

Select a single style of ribbon to use throughout the house or choose several in complementary shades or patterns to edge a lampshade, make a treetop bow, trim a picture frame, or make a ribbon rose.

I'll tell you how

the Sun rose

A Ribbon

at a time.

— Emily Dickinson

Ribbon Care

Ribbon can be used again and again if properly cleaned and stored. Unless using ribbon specifically designed for outdoor use, prevent fading or spotting by keeping ribbon out of direct sunlight and avoiding exposure to the elements.

After the holidays carefully untie the bow or undo the shape. Most ribbons can be washed in cool water with a mild soap and then dried flat and pressed gently with a warm iron. Silk ribbon may require professional dry-cleaning.

Rewind the ribbon on a spool for easy storage or roll it around a cardboard tube and wrap it in acid-free tissue paper; store it in a cardboard box. Fine silk ribbons should never be wrapped in plastic or stored in plastic boxes because plastic traps moisture and could cause the fabric to mildew or deteriorate.

Ribbon-Wrapped Shades

For the large square lampshade pictured opposite, begin at 1 corner and use a hot-glue gun and glue sticks to glue ribbon around the top and bottom edges of the shade. Dab the ends of the ribbon with glue and fold them under for neatness.

Lace the ribbon at the corners of the shade. On both sides of each corner, measure and mark 1" from the top and bottom of the shade; then measure and mark 2" from the top and bottom of the shade. Use a craft knife to carefully cut a hole in the shade at each mark. Like lacing a shoe, lace the ribbon through the holes, beginning at the bottom corner of the shade and tying a bow at the top corner.

For the small chandelier or candle shades, wrap the shade with ⅛" satin ribbon and add a braided trim around the top and bottom. Use a spray adhesive to attach the ⅛" ribbon. Spray the adhesive heavily onto a paper-covered surface or plate. Dip a cotton swab into the adhesive and spread the adhesive in a 1" strip around the shade. Starting at the seam, wind the ribbon around the shade, holding the end of the ribbon and pulling tightly. Slightly overlap the ribbon as you wrap it around.

Repeat this procedure to cover the shade, using different colors of ribbon as desired. Be sure to cut the ribbon at the seam of the shade. Use a hot-glue gun and glue sticks to attach the braided trim around the top and bottom of the shade.

Ribbon Photo Mats

Before you begin, decide on the mat size (we covered 8" x 10" and 5" x 7" mats), ribbons, and pattern you desire.

Measure and cut the ribbons to cover each side of the mat. Using craft glue, secure each piece of ribbon to the mat, beginning at the outside edges and working toward the inside.

As you attach each ribbon piece, cut the ribbon ends at an angle to match the mitered corners of the mat.

Let the glue dry before you place the mat in a frame.

Rounds of narrow silk ribbon encircle charming little candle shades; an ivory lampshade is laced at the corners with satin ribbon.

*A round the base
of a floral-filled
bowl lies a
garland of ribboned
flowers fashioned
from rich satin,
iridescent organza,
and delicate
moiré ribbons.*

Ribbon Roses

To make a flower, use an 18" piece
of 1½"-wide wire-edged ribbon.
Grasp the wire at the bottom edge
of 1 end of the ribbon and gently
pull. As you pull, slip the fabric
along the wire until half of the
edge is gathered. Then grasp the
same wire at the other end of the
ribbon and pull it until the
remaining half of the edge is
gathered. Carefully coil the ribbon
into a cone, grasping the gathered
edges in 1 hand and coiling
the ribbon with the other
(Diagram 1). Secure the gathered
edges of the ribbon with a few
stitches and trim the excess wire.

To make each leaf, use a 3"
piece of 1"-wide wire-edged ribbon. Fold the ribbon in half
lengthwise. Gather the raw edges
by making a running stitch and
pulling on the thread (Diagram
2). Stitch each leaf onto the the
bottom of the rose (Diagram 3).

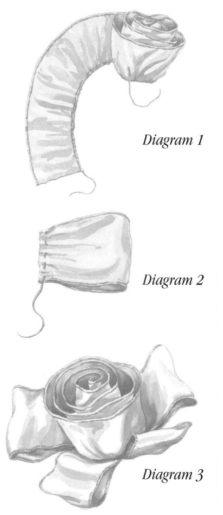

Diagram 1

Diagram 2

Diagram 3

Woven-Ribbon Ornament

*Three colors of ribbons are woven
together to form a basket ornament
to hang on the tree or doorknob.*

You will need (for 1 ornament):
3 different colors of ribbon (1 yard
each of first 2 colors and 1½ yards of
third color); ruler; craft knife; small
piece of cardboard; lightweight
fusible interfacing; straight pins;
tracing paper; ornament pattern on
page 138; ⅓ yard matching fabric;
½ yard matching cording; and
polyester stuffing.

1. Cut each color of ribbon into 8"
strips.

2. To make a base on which to weave
the ribbon, use a ruler and pencil to
mark an 8" square on the cardboard.
Using a ruler and craft knife, cut out
the base along the marked lines. In the
same manner, also cut an 8" square of
lightweight fusible interfacing.

3. Begin weaving the ribbons. If you
use velvet or brocade ribbon that is
decorated on 1 side only, weave the
ribbons with the wrong side up. Pin
the ends of the first 2 colors of ribbon strips to the edges of the base,
alternating colors, until the base is
covered (Diagram at right).

4. Beginning at 1 corner, weave
1 strip of the third color of ribbon
over and under the horizontal
ribbons, pinning the ribbon ends to
secure. Then weave another strip of
the third color, weaving under and
over the alternate horizontal ribbons

(Diagram below). Pin the ends. Continue weaving strips of the third color ribbon in this manner, alternating over and under, until the base is covered. Adjust the ribbons so they are as tightly woven as possible, removing and reinserting pins as necessary.

5. Following the interfacing instructions, use an iron to fuse the interfacing to the woven ribbons. Remove the pins and base.

6. Using tracing paper, transfer the ornament pattern onto the interfacing and cut it out. Repeat, cutting the pattern from fabric for the back of the ornament. Cut a 14" piece of cording.

7. At the marked dots on the pattern, pin the cording ends to the right side of the fabric. With the right sides facing and raw edges aligned, stitch the woven-ribbon front and fabric back together along top and sides, leaving the bottom open. Clip curves and turn the fabric right side out.

8. Fill the ornament as desired with polyester stuffing. Slipstitch the opening closed. (For slipstitch instructions, see page 139.)

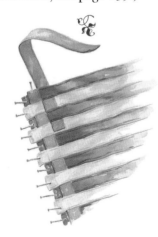

Velvet and embroidered ribbons are woven into a small basket and suspended from the doorknob with a length of silk cord. A sheer green bow catches the light.

Floral Greetings

*Dried flowers are a welcome gift
from the spring and summer garden.*

In winter the growing season seems so far away. That's why flowers and herbs picked at their prime and dried over time are such welcome holiday decorations.

If you plan ahead, your spring and summer harvest will have more than enough time to dry properly by Christmas. If not, florists offer many varieties of already-dried flowers and herbs, as well as a bounty of fresh flowers suitable for quick drying. Where the climate allows, some herbs grow year-round to provide a reliable source for holiday decorating.

Though fresh flowers last longest when cut early in the day, flowers destined to be dried should be picked at midday, after the sun has taken away the dew. (See "Drying Flowers" on page 44 for a list of flowers suitable for drying.)

For air-drying choose an arid place to hang the flowers upside down in small bunches of 3 to 5 stems. Tie the stems together with yarn or string and suspend the bunch from a clothes-drying rack or clothes hangers. Let the blossoms hang for 2 weeks and then check their progress. When they are completely dry, store the flowers between layers of tissue paper in a roomy cardboard box.

Blooms with layered petals dry best with the aid of a dessicant such as silica gel, available as a commercial preparation. This allows a rapid drying time and better preservation of shapes and colors.

To dry flowers by this method, cut off all but 1" of each stem. Pour a 1" layer of silica gel into a container with a snug-fitting lid. Place multi-petaled flowers faceup in the gel or single-petaled flowers facedown. Lay buds or long-stemmed flowers, such as snapdragons, lengthwise in the container. Then gently cover the blossoms with silica gel. Work carefully, for the flowers will assume the shape in which they are positioned. Cover the container and check the progress after 3 days. Properly dried flowers should feel crisp, not brittle. Plants left too long in silica gel will crumble.

Dried flowers and herbs work beautifully in mixed arrangements, dramatic groupings of a single color, or simple clusters of 1 bloom, such as hydrangea or zinnia. They can also be shaped into a colorful swag to be used on a mantel or as a centerpiece.

Clusters of grapes are a creative addition to a mantel swag crafted from everlasting herbs and cut flowers. Note the variety of colors here for an attractive composition.

Flower-Lover's Swag

For a swag similar to the one above, artfully combine bright flowering herbs, fresh or dried flowers, fruits, and seasonal greens.

You will need: Aluminum foil; chicken wire; several florist's foam bricks; florist's wire; dried herbs, such as marjoram, rudbeckia, lavender, rosemary, and sage; dried flowers, such as roses, celosia, heather, hollyhocks, and lady's mantle; seasonal fruits; and greenery, such as cedar or boxwood.

1. Cut foil and chicken wire to desired length of the swag. Stack the foil on the chicken wire. Position the foam bricks on the foil so the foil is about 1½" larger on all sides than the foam.

2. Fold foil around all sides of the foam to form a tray to hold debris. Fold the chicken wire around the foam and foil; secure the ends with florist's wire.

3. Bunch several sprigs of the herbs, flowers, and greenery together and wrap the stems with florist's wire. Press the stems through the chicken wire and into the florist's foam. (If you want to add fresh flowers to the arrangement, secure the flower stems in florist's water vials and tuck them amongst the dried flowers.) Repeat to cover the swag, working from the ends toward the center.

Drying Flowers

These flowers are suited to air drying: artemisia, baby's breath, cockscomb, delphinium, globe amaranth, globe thistle, heather, hydrangea, lady's mantle, lamb's ears, larkspur, lavender, starflower, statice, strawflower, and yarrow.

These flowers hold their shape and color better with dessicant drying: dahlia, daisy, delphinium, dogwood, lilac, marigold, oregano in bloom, peony, rose, snapdragon, and zinnia.

A bounty of everlastings, this wreath is an exuberant mix of rosebuds, eucalyptus, baby's breath, berries, and statice.

Chapter II

Gifts

Handmade keepsakes, heartfelt greetings, and
beautifully wrapped presents—here you'll find
a gift for everyone on your Christmas list.

Handmade Messages

Let a handmade card express your holiday wishes.

When you need a small heartfelt gift, a beautiful custom-made card is ideal. You'll find it is a pleasure to tailor the design to the recipient. Begin with a purchased blank ivory or white card and decorate it with stamps, ribbons, sealing wax, or pressed greenery.

Decorate the front of a card using a favorite holiday stamp with metallic or brightly colored ink. Or use black ink and enhance the design with colored pencils or watercolors.

Lace a ribbon through two holes punched at the top of the card and tie the ribbon in a bow. Or tie the ribbon as a card closure, lacing it through holes punched on each side of the card opening.

Pressed flowers and sprigs of greenery grace cards with natural beauty. Fern-frond tips become miniature Christmas trees when attached to a card with spray adhesive. Add the name and origin of the plant or some other sentiment to the card.

The best cordial is to read

over all the letters of one's friends.

— William Shenstone

Create an imaginative collection of cards adorned with stamps, wax seals, and greenery.

For ease and room for error, first make the wax seal on waxed paper. When the wax has hardened, peel the seal from the paper and glue it to the card or envelope.

Wax Seals

Add a regal flourish to a card by using a wax stamp with your initial, recipient's initial, or motif of your choosing. To make the wax seal, wave the end of a wax stick through the flame of a butane lighter. Be careful: the wax can ignite. Drip the melted wax directly onto the card or onto a piece of waxed paper or foil. When the melted wax circle is almost as large as the stamp you have chosen, press the stamp into the wax and hold it there until the wax has begun to cool.

If you made the impression on waxed paper or foil, let the wax cool and harden completely before carefully peeling it away from the paper or foil. Glue the wax seal into position on the card.

For a gilded look, press the stamp in metallic ink before stamping the wax.

Imprinted Velvet

With a simple technique, a favorite fabric dons your personal touch.

Remember your first velvet dress? Nothing felt prettier or more grown-up than the rich folds of its silky softness beneath your fingertips.

When printed with a beautiful design, velvet acquires even more sophistication, which suits it for holiday giving. Create imprinted velvet by heat-pressing a rubber stamp onto the fabric. Stitch the imprinted fabric into luxurious items for giving—or for keeping.

Imprinted Velvet

For the most dramatic imprint, be sure to use a rayon or silk velvet instead of a cotton or washable velvet.

You will need: Rayon, rayon-acetate, or silk velvet in desired yardage; water in a spray bottle; rubber stamp with a bold design; and ironing board and iron.

1. To imprint the velvet, generously mist the right side of the velvet with water. Place the stamp, rubber side up, on an ironing board. Lay the dampened fabric, right side down, on top of the rubber stamp.

2. Set the iron on the wool setting. Do not use steam. When the iron has warmed to the proper temperature, press the velvet on top of the stamp. Hold the iron firmly in place for approximately 20 seconds. If the image is not as distinct as you would like, press the fabric onto the stamp for an additional 10 seconds.

3. Continue imprinting the pattern onto the fabric in this manner to complete the desired design.

Rose-Covered Shawl

For a gracious gift that shows off the stamped designs, stitch together two rectangles of velvet, adding a coordinating trim around the edge.

You will need: 2⅛ yards imprinted velvet (approximately 48" wide); 4¾ yards matching fringe; matching thread; and straight pins.

Note: The finished size of this shawl is 35" x 44". All seam allowances are ½".

1. Cut 2 (37" x 46") rectangles of velvet, rounding the corners. With a sewing machine, zigzag or serge the raw edges to make handling the velvet easier.

2. To add the trim to 1 velvet piece, on a sewing machine, lengthen the stitch length and loosen the presser foot tension. With the right sides facing, align the top edge of the fringe with the edges of the velvet, securing the fringe with straight pins. Stitch the fringe in place around the edges. Trim the excess fringe so that the beginning and ending edges meet after stitching.

3. With the right sides facing, edges aligned, and fringe to the inside, pin the velvet pieces together. Stitching along the previous stitching line, stitch the 2 pieces together, leaving an 8" opening for turning. Turn the shawl right side out and slipstitch the opening closed. (For slipstitch instructions, see page 139.)

4. If you need to press the shawl, hold the iron over—but do not touch—the velvet. Let the steam penetrate any wrinkles.

*This velvet shawl displays
its glowing rose imprints.*

A nosegay of red roses inspired the design on this velvet bag.

Velvet Gift Bag

A soft drawstring bag is superb for presenting a small gift.

You will need: ¼ yard imprinted velvet (approximately 48" wide); matching thread; and 1½ yards cording.

Note: All seam allowances are ½".

1. From the velvet, cut 2 (9" x 14") rectangular pieces. Cut a 6"-diameter circle for the bottom of the bag. With a sewing machine, zigzag or serge the raw edges to make handling the velvet easier.

2. With the right sides together and edges aligned, stitch the velvet rectangles together. Fold 1 short edge 3" to the wrong side and topstitch it in place along the inside edge of the zigzag stitch. Topstitch again ½" from the inside edge of the zigzag stitching and previous topstitching. This creates a casing for the drawstring.

3. With the right sides facing and edges aligned, stitch the velvet circle to the rectangles. Turn the bag right side out.

4. Cut the cording into 2 (22"-long) pieces. Using a seam ripper, cut a few stitches from each side seam of the casing for an opening for the drawstring. Insert 1 end of 1 cording piece into 1 side of 1 seam opening. Thread the cording through the casing until the cording end comes out of the other side of the same seam opening. Knot the cording ends together. Repeat with the remaining cording piece, threading it through the remaining seam opening.

Let us crown ourselves with rosebuds...

Let us leave tokens of our joyfulness in every place.

— *Apocrypha*

Gifts of Velvet

With imagination and basic sewing skills, you can create many gifts from imprinted velvet.

• *Stitch a velvet Christmas stocking and imprint the recipient's monogram on the cuff.*

• *Cover a Christmas photo album.*

• *Make a runner for the sideboard or stitch slipcovers for sofa pillows.*

• *Place a small gift in the center of a scrap of the velvet, pull the corners up, and tie with a pretty ribbon.*

A colorful floral band bordered with a berry design surrounds this felt topper.

Christmas Chapeaux

Jaunty hatbands lend a jolly holiday accent.

Hats embody charm and practicality, flattering the wearer while chasing away the winter chill during a sleigh ride or while out caroling. A hat-lover will enjoy a plush felt topper with a colorful band hand-stitched by you.

Cross-stitched Hatbands

To customize our cross-stitch designs on the following pages, choose different colors of embroidery floss and linen.

You will need (for 1 hatband): ½ yard 32-count linen; embroidery floss as specified on cross-stitch pattern; needle; desired cross-stitch pattern, page 58; and matching thread.

1. Measure the circumference of the hat.

2. Following the cross-stitch chart, cross-stitch the design, repeating the pattern to a length equal to or ¼" shorter than the hat circumference.

3. Centering the cross-stitch pattern, trim the fabric width to 4½". Centering the pattern, cut the fabric length to the hat circumference plus 1", allowing a ½" seam allowance at each end.

4. To mark the top edge, fold the fabric to the wrong side as desired along the top edge of the cross-stitch pattern. Press the fold.

5. Fold the 4½" strip of fabric in half lengthwise, with the right sides facing. Stitch a ½" seam along the length of the fabric. Finger-press the seam open. Turn the fabric right side out and press the folds.

6. At 1 end, fold the ½" seam allowance to the inside. Press the fold. Insert the opposite end into the tube and pin it in place. Position the band on the hat and adjust the length of the band as necessary. Remove the band and slipstitch the ends together. (For slipstitch instructions, see page 139.)

7. Place the finished hatband on the hat and tack the band to the hat to hold it in place, if desired.

Gifts to Stitch

These versatile cross-stitch motifs are designed in a continuous pattern, making them easy to adapt for other gift ideas.

• *Trim the cuff of a pair of gloves or mittens or decorate the edge of a pillowcase.*

• *Add the holiday border to purchased linen or cotton towels for hostess gifts.*

• *Stitch a design along the collar or cuff of a linen blouse or at the hem of a nightgown or apron.*

Floral Pattern

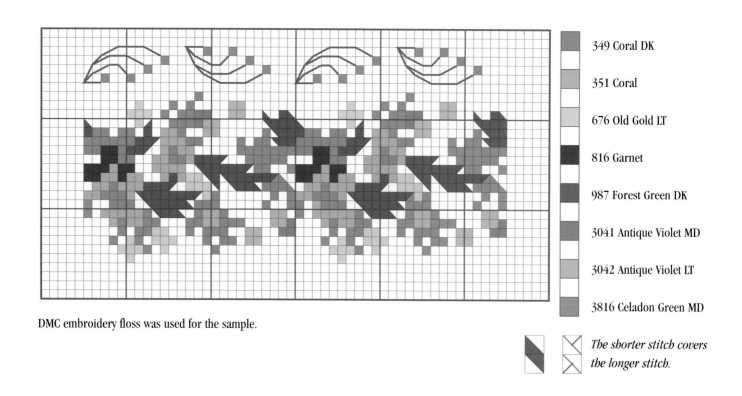

DMC embroidery floss was used for the sample.

349 Coral DK

351 Coral

676 Old Gold LT

816 Garnet

987 Forest Green DK

3041 Antique Violet MD

3042 Antique Violet LT

3816 Celadon Green MD

The shorter stitch covers the longer stitch.

Trumpet and Holly Pattern

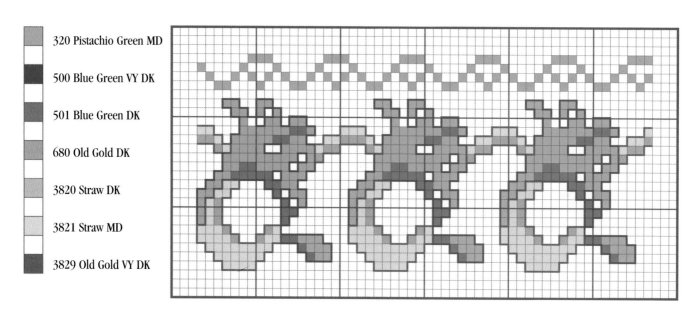

320 Pistachio Green MD

500 Blue Green VY DK

501 Blue Green DK

680 Old Gold DK

3820 Straw DK

3821 Straw MD

3829 Old Gold VY DK

DMC embroidery floss was used for the sample.

Signaling the season, this hat wears a red band stitched with a trumpet and holly motif.

*A paper doily makes a
striking package topper: place
a lacy doily onto a gift wrapped
in a solid color paper. Or fold a
square doily into an envelope
to hold a small flat gift.*

Memorable Wraps

Wrap even the simplest gift with a sense of holiday magic.

Imaginative wrapping gives each gift an extra measure of love and care.
Use paper doilies, scrap fabrics, and handmade papers in unexpected ways to create
one-of-a-kind packages for everyone on your list. Here are a few ideas.

Paper-Doily Wraps

For a lacy effect, tape square, round, or rectangular paper doilies around gifts wrapped in solid paper. Weave ribbon through the holes in a doily and tie it in a bow. Fold a square doily's corners to its center and glue 3 of the 4 in place for a custom envelope to hold a photo, poem, or sketch.

Fabric Envelopes

Create fabric envelopes to hold photos, tickets, lace, or jewelry. For a pattern, unfold a paper envelope and trace its shape onto 2 pieces of scrap fabric and a piece of lightweight fusible web. Following the manufacturer's instructions for the fusible web, fuse the web onto the wrong side of the fabric piece intended for the outside of the envelope. Remove the paper backing from the fusible web and fuse the outside fabric to the remaining fabric piece (the envelope lining).

Using an intact paper envelope as a guide, fold the side flaps toward the center. Then fold the bottom flap up. Secure the bottom flap to the side flaps, using strips of fusible web. Trim the envelopes with cording and fabric-covered buttons.

Transform scrap fabrics into envelopes to give antique laces, buttons, or photos.

Natural handmade papers and raffia wrap luxurious French soaps.

Natural Wraps

Enhance a purchased set of French-milled soaps by wrapping them in floral handmade paper. Add a raffia bow with a bit of greenery, dried rosebuds, or sprigs of lavender. Present the soaps in an antique silver dish tied with a bow of silk ribbon.

Custom-made Paper

Create your own wrapping paper, choosing a bold, simple design stamped or stenciled onto solid paper. Secure ribbon with a large wax seal or large whimsical button.

Tulle-Covered Boxes

For a feminine touch on a small gift, cut a square of tulle or lace and place the gift in the center. Pull the fabric up around the gift and tie it up with a ribbon bow. Attach a sprig of greenery, kept fresh in a florist's vial filled with water.

Top a purchased set of soaps with dried roses or lavender sprigs to give a hint of the soap's fragrance.

With its lacy tulle covering, this gift is almost too pretty to open.

Sure to be a cherished gift, a handkerchief linen pillow is marked by a monogram of beads. To make this pillow, see page 66 for the instructions.

Monogrammed linens are valued gifts and collectibles. With special care and cleaning, they can be enjoyed for years (see Caring for Linens *below).*

Initial Impressions

The art of monogramming adds a meaningful touch.

Though monogramming began as a practical method of identifying ownership of possessions, it has become a thoughtful way to personalize a gift, too. From a single letter on a fine linen handkerchief to elaborately embroidered tracings on towels and tea services, a monogram signals that the gift was made especially for the recipient.

A monogrammed gift is not only a lovely idea at Christmas but also offers a classic and beautiful way to welcome a new member into the family or mark a significant occasion any time of the year. At left, a crisp white linen pillow is branded with a beaded monogram.

Caring for Linens

To keep your antique or new linens in excellent condition, clean and store them with care.

• To remove stains, act quickly: stains are easier to remove when they have just occurred. To avoid spreading the stain, always dab at the outer edges of the stain first and then move toward the center. Never rub the stain.

• Press linens while they are damp, stretching them into shape before ironing. Iron linens first on the wrong side to eliminate creases and water marks. Then iron on the right side to enhance the sheen. Tumbling linens in the clothes dryer tends to overdry them.

• To store linens, wrap them in blue tissue paper for protection from light damage. White tissue lets light penetrate, causing yellowing. Place linens on slatted shelves to allow air to circulate, avoiding dampness or excessive heat.

Beaded Monogram Pillow

A single initial is stitched with beads on handkerchief linen.

You will need: ½ yard 45"-wide handkerchief linen; ¼ yard 45"-wide cotton organdy; matching thread; embroidery hoop; monogram stitch chart, page 67; beading needle; 2 (4.5-gram) packages pearl seed beads; and pillow form to fit.

Note: The finished size of the pillow is 16" x 20". All seam allowances are ½".

1. From the linen, cut 2 (17" x 21") pieces and 1 (10" x 17") piece. Set aside 1 large piece and the small piece for the pillow back. From the organdy, cut 4 (3" x 22") strips.

2. Fold the remaining large linen piece in quarters to find the center. Baste along the crease lines to mark the center. Using the embroidery hoop and following the monogram stitch chart, stitch the beads in the desired monogram pattern at the center of the linen piece. Measure and baste a 5" x 7" box around the monogram. Stitch 2 rows of beads along the basting lines to make the box. (For basting stitch instructions, see page 139.) Carefully press the monogrammed piece.

3. With a sewing machine, zigzag along 1 short edge of each pillow back piece. Turn the zigzagged edge under 2" on the small piece and 4" on the large piece. Press the folds.

4. With the right sides facing and raw edges aligned, place the large pillow back piece on top of the monogrammed piece. Place the small pillow back piece right side down on top of the large pillow back piece, aligning the short raw edge with the remaining short raw edge of the monogrammed piece. The folded edges of the back pieces will overlap approximately 2".

5. Stitch all the pieces together along the raw edges. Press. Turn the pillow cover right side out, positioning the seams on edge and pressing again.

Using the cross-stitch patterns at right, stitch the pearl beads to form the desired letters.

6. To make the pillow flange, pin the pillow cover along the seams to secure. Baste 2" from the outer edges, forming the flange.

7. To make the organdy flange overlay, on 1 long edge of each organdy strip, stitch ¼" from the edge. Turn the raw edges under along this stitching. Arrange the strips around the pillow flange, placing the turned edge ¼" off the outer edge of the pillow. Miter the corners of the organdy strips and pin to mark. Remove the strips from the pillow.

8. Stitch the mitered corners together. Turn the outer edge under ¼" again and stitch to hem.

9. Place the organdy flange overlay on top of the pillow, aligning the hemmed edge of the organdy with the finished edge of the pillow. Align the mitered seams of the organdy with the corners of the basting stitches, creating the flange.

10. On 1 side, turn the organdy right side down and stitch the organdy to the pillow, following the basting stitches for the flange. Repeat to stitch the remaining organdy sides to the flange. Trim the raw edges of the organdy to ¼". Press the organdy overlay flat. Topstitch the organdy to the pillow ¼" from the stitching line, enclosing the raw edge in the seam.

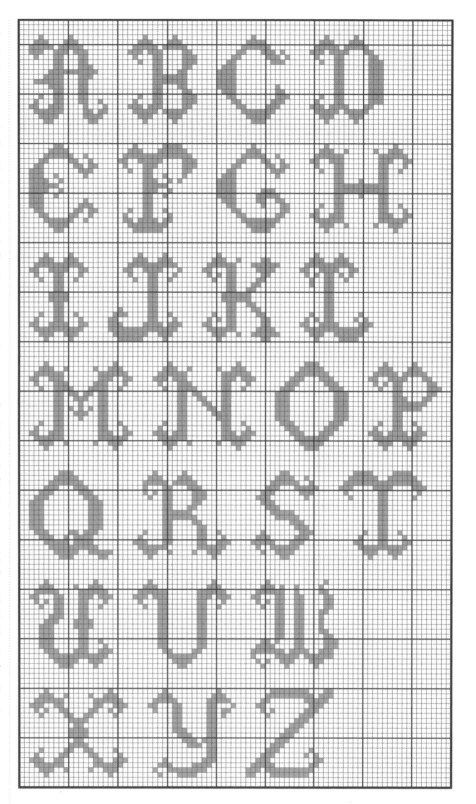

The Season for Scarves

*As warm as a Christmas wish, pretty scarves
are perennial favorites.*

A winter necessity becomes a joy to wear when you've graced it with your handwork. A cozy muffler is easy to make, especially when you begin with a purchased wool scarf and tailor the trimmings to the recipient's style.

Delicate lace adds a feminine accent to a traditional tartan, and a generous length of silky black velvet gains a ruffled band of red plaid taffeta. A winter white scarf dotted with tiny pearls is certainly suited for elegant evenings.

Present a handmade scarf in a pretty hatbox and add a card with tips for wearing and caring. Take special pride in knowing that your gift symbolizes the warmth of love and friendship.

Appliquéd Lace Scarf

Pristine lace ribbon romances a plaid wool scarf.

You will need: Purchased scarf (scarf at right measures 12" x 60"); 2 yards 4"-wide lace ribbon (or 6 times the width of the scarf, plus 3"); and thread to match the lace.

1. Cut 3 (23"-long) strips of lace or 3 pieces of lace twice the width of the scarf, plus 1".

2. Beginning at 1 side edge of the scarf, pin the lace horizontally across the front and back of the scarf or as desired. (We covered the plaid woven into the scarf at the ends and in the middle.) Where the ends of each lace strip meet, fold the lace ¼" over the edge of the scarf to the other side. Turn under the raw edge of this end of lace to cover the beginning raw edge of the lace. Pin the ends of the lace in place.

3. Appliqué the lace to scarf. Slipstitch through the lace to hide the stitches. (For slipstitch instructions, see page 139.)

A cheerful tartan wool scarf boasts an appliqué of snow white lace.

This winter white scarf wears handstitched pearl beads.

Beaded Winter White Scarf

A scattering of pearl beads makes this camel-hair scarf even more luxurious.

You will need: Purchased scarf; 4-mm pearl beads (we used approximately 180 beads); matching thread; and beading needle.

Before you begin, plan the desired bead pattern for the scarf. Stitch each bead to the right side of the scarf as desired. On the scarf at left, the beads are stitched in a pyramid shape at each end of the scarf (approximately 90 beads are stitched on each end). Near the middle of the scarf, the beads are stitched close together to form the point of the pyramid; then they are stitched farther apart toward the end of the scarf, giving the beads the appearance of raining down each end of the scarf.

In holiday colors, taffeta ruffles finish the ends of this black velvet scarf.

Velvet and Tartan Scarf

With its holiday taffeta ruffle, this scarf is made to wear at Christmas. If you prefer, finish the ends with a ruffle from another color of fabric to match the recipient's style.

You will need: ¾ yard 54"-wide black velvet; ⅝ yard tartan plaid taffeta; and matching thread.

Note: The finished size of the scarf is 11½" x 57". All seam allowances are ½".

1. Cut 2 (13" x 54") pieces from the velvet. Cut 2 (5"-wide) bias strips from the taffeta.

2. Fold 1 taffeta strip lengthwise, with the wrong sides together. Square off the ends, leaving a strip approximately 24" long. Stitch along the short ends. Turn the strip right side out and press. Repeat with the remaining taffeta strip.

3. Using a running or gathering stitch, stitch 2 gathering rows ¼" and ½" from the raw edge along the length of each taffeta strip. To gather each strip, gently pull the threads. Gather each strip to measure 12" long.

4. Pin the taffeta ruffles at each end on the right side of 1 velvet piece, aligning the raw edges and leaving a ½" seam allowance along each long side of the velvet piece. Stitch each ruffle to the velvet along the ½" gathering row.

5. With the right sides facing, raw edges aligned, and ruffles to the inside, stitch the 2 velvet pieces together, leaving an 8" opening along 1 long side for turning.

6. Turn the scarf right side out and slipstitch the opening closed.

Gift boxes wrapped in colorful fabrics wait under the Christmas tree to be opened.

Beautiful Boxes

A box wrapped with fine fabrics or papers becomes a special carryall.

Everyone who needs a place to store their treasures and necessities—handkerchiefs, hair ribbons, love letters—will appreciate the results of your time and care.

Begin with a hatbox, square box, or shoe box. Cover it with remnants of new or vintage fabrics, wallpapers, and ribbons. Select a unifying color scheme but don't be afraid to mix patterns and textures. Perhaps use one fabric for the lid and a complementary fabric for the base. Line the inside of the base and lid with paper and, for extra softness, pad the lid before covering. Finish the box with silk cording and secure the lid with organdy ribbon; tuck in a sprig of holly or ivy.

Fabric-Covered Boxes

Choose boxes with loose-fitting lids to accommodate the fabric. You can use these instructions to cover boxes with papers as well.

You will need (for 1 round box): Desired box; assorted fabrics; and craft glue or spray adhesive.

1. Measure the diameter of the bottom of the box and add 2" to the measurement. Cut the desired fabric to fit. Center and glue the fabric to the bottom of the box so that 1" overlaps all the way around. Clip the edges of the fabric and glue the clipped edges to the side of the box.

2. Measure the height and circumference of the box and add 2" to each measurement. Cut the desired fabric to fit. Fold the bottom raw edge under 1" and glue the fabric around the side of the box. Where the ends meet, overlap the raw edges, folding the overlapping edge under 1" before gluing in place (Diagram 1). Fold the top raw edge over the box rim and glue the fabric to the inside of the box.

Diagram 1

3. Measure the diameter of the lid and add 2" to the measurement. Cut the desired fabric to fit. Center and glue the fabric to the lid so that 1" overlaps all the way around. Clip the edges of the fabric and glue the clipped edges to the side of the lid (Diagram 2).

Diagram 2

4. Measure the circumference and height of the lid. Cut the desired fabric to fit. Fold the top raw edge under and glue the fabric around the side of the lid (Diagram 3). Where the ends meet, overlap the raw edges, folding the overlapping edge under 1" before gluing in place. Fold the bottom raw edge under and glue the fabric to the inside of the box lid.

Diagram 3

5. Place the lid on the box base.

Evergreen Gestures

*An embroidered cushion is filled with evergreens
to capture the season's scent.*

A miniature keepsake sachet is a fresh, fragrant gift of nature. Fill a handmade sachet with needles and small clippings from the Christmas tree or regional evergreens enhanced with a few drops of essential evergreen oil.

Begin this project at any time during the year and finish just before Christmas so the evergreens are fresh. Stitch the sachets in fabrics to suit the recipient's decor, adding pieces of lace and braid or a seasonal cross-stitched motif. Embroider a monogram or date. Or have family members sign their names on the fabric and embroider over the script.

Evergreen Keepsake Sachets

Let your imagination and the recipient be your guide as you decorate the sachets. We personalized ours with ribbon-embroidered pinecones, monograms, and family names.

You will need (for 2 sachets): ¼ yard 45"-wide douppioni; ¼ yard muslin; silk ribbon in desired color; embroidery floss in desired color; embroidery needle; 1 yard upholstery trim or lace; and desired evergreen clippings to fill the finished sachet.

Note: The finished size of each sachet is 8" square. All seam allowances are ½". For embroidery stitch instructions, see page 76.

1. From the douppioni, cut 2 (9") squares. From the muslin, cut 2 (9") squares.

2. Using silk ribbon and embroidery floss, decorate 1 fabric square as desired for the sachet front.

3. On the white sachet at right, the pinecones are created with a Cretan stitch, using silk ribbon. The pine needles are made with a split stitch and straight stitch, using embroidery floss. To create the initial, use a stem stitch and silk ribbon to trace over an initial pattern or initial signed onto the fabric.

4. To stitch the signatures on the green sachet (see page 77), use a stem stitch and embroidery floss to trace over the signatures signed onto the fabric. Add lace appliqués to the corners of the sachet front fabric, slipstitching the edges of the lace to the fabric. (For slipstitch instructions, see page 139.)

5. With the right sides together and raw edges aligned, stitch the sachet front to the sachet back along 3 sides, inserting the upholstery trim into the seam before stitching, if necessary. Whipstitch the trim to the sachet front at the opening. (For whipstitch instructions, see page 139.) Turn the sachet right side out. Press the seams in place.

6. With the right sides together and raw edges aligned, stitch the muslin squares together along 3 sides. Turn the pieces right side out. Press the seams in place. Fill the muslin bag with evergreen clippings until the bag is firm. Slipstitch the opening closed.

7. Insert the evergreen-filled muslin bag into the sachet. Slipstitch the opening closed.

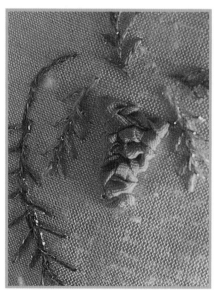

Strands of metallic thread add luster to the embroidered pine needles that surround the silk ribbon pinecones.

Silk ribbon and embroidery floss beautify this keepsake with stitched pinecones and evergreen needles—a clue to what the sachet holds.

Embroidery

Threading and Knotting

To anchor a length of silk ribbon to the needle, pierce the ribbon end (A) and slide it down the needle to lock it in place (B).

To knot the remaining silk ribbon end, bring the ribbon end up to the point of the needle (C). Make a running stitch in the ribbon end (D) and gently pull the needle and ribbon through the running stitch to form a knot.

Stem Stitch

Come up at A, go down at B, and come up again at C. Repeat to complete the desired design.

Straight Stitch

Come up at A, go down at B, and come up again at C. Repeat to complete the desired design, varying the stitch length as needed.

Split Stitch

Come up at A and go down at B. Split the ribbon or floss in the middle as the needle comes up at C; go down at D. Repeat to complete the desired design, varying the stitch length as needed.

Cretan Stitch

Come up at A and go down at B, making a straight stitch. Come up at C. Take the ribbon over the A-B stitch and go down over and under the stitch at D. Bring the needle back over the A-B stitch and go under at E, coming up and through the loop in the ribbon. Take the needle under the C-D stitch at F and come up through the loop in the ribbon. Continue E and F until the A-B and C-D stitches are covered.

To personalize the sachet, have family members sign the fabric and then embroider over their signatures, using a stem stitch.

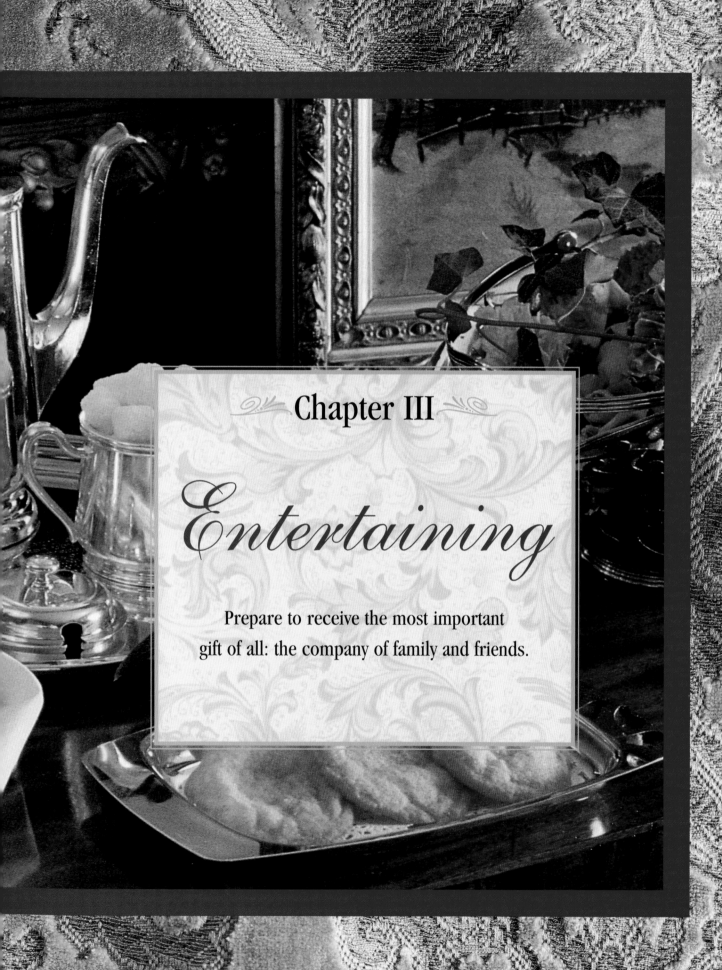

Chapter III

Entertaining

Prepare to receive the most important
gift of all: the company of family and friends.

At the Hearth

Let a crackling fire set the mood and add warmth
to your next Christmas gathering.

An afternoon tea, an exchange of gifts, or perhaps a champagne toast to the arrival of family and friends—all will be made memorable when you celebrate at the hearth.

This is the time for candlelight, delicious food and drink, and sinking into your most comfortable chairs, for you want this time to last forever. Let the menu be as luxurious as the moment.

Menu

Bakewell Tart

Pavé Tart

*Chocolate-Dipped
Strawberries*

*Champagne
Coffee
Tea*

Bakewell Tart

*A buttery, flaky crust surrounds a
filling flavored with raspberry jam
and ground almonds and blanketed
with a sweet, creamy glaze.*

PÂTE BRISÉE:
2   cups all-purpose flour
2   teaspoons sugar
1   teaspoon salt
14 tablespoons unsalted butter, cut
       into small pieces
1   large egg
1   tablespoon milk

FILLING:
½   cup raspberry jam
4   tablespoons unsalted butter,
       softened
4½ tablespoons sugar
1   large egg
⅔   cup ground almonds (2 ounces)
1   cup pound cake crumbs (2 ounces)
½   teaspoon almond extract

CONFECTIONERS' SUGAR GLAZE:
2   tablespoons unsalted butter
1   cup confectioners' sugar
2   tablespoons whipping cream
1   teaspoon vanilla extract
Fresh strawberries for garnish

TO MAKE PÂTE BRISÉE:
1. Position the knife blade in a food processor bowl; add the 2 cups flour, 2 teaspoons sugar, salt, and 14 tablespoons butter. Pulse until the mixture resembles fine crumbs.
2. In a small bowl, whisk together the 1 egg and milk until blended. With the processor running, pour in the egg mixture, processing until the dough pulls away from the sides of the bowl and forms a ball.
3. Divide the dough in half. Form each half into a disk shape. Wrap separately in plastic wrap and chill at least 30 minutes.
4. On a floured surface, roll out half the dough. Fit onto a 7" tart pan with a removable bottom. (Chill remaining half of the pastry for another use.)

TO MAKE FILLING:
1. Spread the jam in the bottom of the unbaked pastry shell.
2. In a small mixer bowl, beat the 4 tablespoons butter and 4½ tablespoons sugar at medium speed of an electric mixer until thick and white. Beat in the egg, ground almonds, cake crumbs, and almond extract.
3. Spoon the filling in small mounds all over the jam; spread evenly. Place the tart on a baking sheet.
4. Bake at 350° for 30 to 40 minutes or until puffed and set in the center.

TO MAKE GLAZE:
1. While the tart is baking, in a saucepan, melt the 2 tablespoons butter. Remove from heat and sift in the confectioners' sugar. Stir in the cream and vanilla until smooth.
2. Spread the glaze over the piping hot tart. Cool in the pan on a wire rack.
3. Garnish with fresh strawberries.
       Yield: one 7" tart.

Silver serving pieces reflect the flickering firelight, which casts an intimate glow over a low table set for dessert.

An inviting display of china cups and crystal flutes near the gleaming hearth signals that the occasion is special.

Pavé Tart

*This impressive dessert is meant
to be sliced and served like cake.*

CAKE:

1	cup unsalted butter, cut into pieces
4	tablespoons unsweetened cocoa powder
1	cup water
2	cups sugar
2	cups all-purpose flour
1	teaspoon ground cinnamon
1	teaspoon baking soda
½	cup buttermilk
2	large eggs, lightly beaten
1	teaspoon vanilla extract

PECAN ICING:

½	cup unsalted butter, cut into pieces
4	tablespoons unsweetened cocoa powder
6	tablespoons milk
4	cups confectioners' sugar
1	teaspoon vanilla extract
1	cup chopped pecans

TO MAKE CAKE:

1. Butter and flour a 13" x 9" x 2" baking pan. Line the bottom of the pan with waxed paper. Butter and flour the waxed paper.
2. In a large saucepan, combine the 1 cup butter, 4 tablespoons cocoa, and 1 cup water. Bring to a boil, stirring to dissolve the cocoa and melt the butter. Remove from heat and set aside.
3. Sift together the sugar, flour, and cinnamon. Gradually stir into the cocoa mixture; mix well. Set aside.
4. Stir the baking soda into the buttermilk. Add the buttermilk mixture, eggs, and vanilla to the cocoa mixture; mix well. Pour into the pan.

5. Bake at 400° for 25 to 30 minutes or until a toothpick inserted in the center comes out clean. Cool in the pan on a wire rack 10 minutes. Remove from the pan. Cool on the wire rack.
6. Cut the cooled cake in thirds lengthwise, making each piece about 2¾" wide and 12" long. Trim the top of each cake piece with a serrated knife so the tops are even. Set the cake pieces aside.

TO MAKE ICING:

1. In a heavy medium saucepan, combine the ½ cup butter, cocoa, and milk. Cook over medium heat, stirring to dissolve the cocoa and melt the butter, forming a smooth mixture. Remove from heat.
2. Gradually sift in the 4 cups confectioners' sugar, beating with a wooden spoon until smooth after each addition.
3. Stir in the 1 teaspoon vanilla and nuts.

TO ASSEMBLE:

Place 1 cake rectangle on a serving plate. Spread with some icing. Continue layering the cake rectangles and icing. Frost the top and sides of the cake. Cut into 1" squares to serve.
Yield: 12 servings.

Note: For easier handling, cut the cake rectangles in half crosswise so the pieces are 6" long. Layer the cake pieces as directed above, making 2 smaller cakes of 3 layers each.

Chocolate-Dipped Strawberries

Choose plump, fresh berries without blemishes; leave their stems intact to facilitate dipping and serving.

12	to 16 large fresh strawberries with stems
4	ounces German sweet chocolate, broken up
¼	cup sugar
¼	cup whipping cream
2	tablespoons unsalted butter
½	teaspoon vanilla extract

1. Wash the strawberries. Pat the berries and caps thoroughly dry with paper towels. Set aside on paper towels.
2. In the top of a double boiler, combine the chocolate, sugar, whipping cream, butter, and vanilla. Stir over simmering water until the chocolate is completely melted and the mixture is smooth.
3. Remove from heat, but leave the chocolate mixture over the hot water in the double boiler.
4. Working quickly, dip the strawberries into the chocolate mixture, swirling until fully coated. Hold the strawberries over the chocolate mixture, letting any excess chocolate mixture drip off.
5. Arrange the strawberries on a baking sheet lined with parchment or waxed paper. Chill until ready to serve.
Yield: 12 to 16.

An architectural marvel, croquembouche (it means "crisp in the mouth" in French) is a towering dessert that can double as a spectacular centerpiece.

Sweet Celebrations

A dessert party is the gourmet's response to visions of sugarplums.

Exquisite desserts are a celebration unto themselves and richly deserving of a solo performance. Invite guests to drop by after any number of holiday events: a matinee of *The Nutcracker,* a church play or pageant, a day of shopping or decorating, or caroling around the neighborhood.

Serve your own tempting sweets or ask guests to bring a beloved recipe from childhood and share its origins at the gathering. Our menu offers a dessert to suit each guest's fancy.

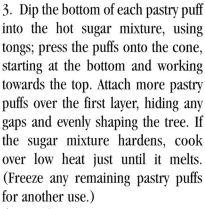

Menu

Croquembouche

White Chocolate Mousse
with Raspberry Sauce

Raspberry and Lemon
Cheesecake

Champagne
Coffee

Croquembouche

Assemble this grand French dessert as close to serving time as possible. Serve by pulling each caramelized-sugar-crowned pastry puff from the others with two forks or silver tongs.

CHOUX PASTRY PUFFS:
3   cups water
1½ cups butter
3   cups all-purpose flour
1½ teaspoons salt
12   large eggs

CARAMELIZED SUGAR:
2   cups sugar
½   cup water
1   cup light corn syrup

TO MAKE PASTRY PUFFS:
1. Bring the 3 cups water and butter to a boil in a large saucepan over medium-high heat; reduce heat to low.
2. Add the flour and salt and beat with a wooden spoon until the mixture leaves the sides of the pan.

Remove from heat and cool slightly.
3. Add the eggs, 1 at a time, beating until smooth.
4. Spoon the batter into a decorating bag fitted with a large star tip; pipe 1½" mounds, 2" apart, onto lightly greased baking sheets (see note).
5. Bake at 450° for 10 minutes; reduce oven temperature to 375° and bake 30 additional minutes or until puffed and golden. Pierce the warm puffs on 1 side with a small sharp knife to let the steam escape. Let cool.
6. Cover a 12" or 15" plastic foam cone with aluminum foil and place on an 18" x 12" piece of foil. Lightly grease the foil.

TO MAKE CARAMELIZED SUGAR:
1. Combine the sugar, ½ cup water, and corn syrup in a heavy saucepan; cook over low heat, stirring constantly, until the sugar melts.
2. Bring to a boil over high heat; cook, stirring constantly, 5 minutes or until the mixture is light amber. Remove from heat; cool 2 minutes or until slightly thickened.

3. Dip the bottom of each pastry puff into the hot sugar mixture, using tongs; press the puffs onto the cone, starting at the bottom and working towards the top. Attach more pastry puffs over the first layer, hiding any gaps and evenly shaping the tree. If the sugar mixture hardens, cook over low heat just until it melts. (Freeze any remaining pastry puffs for another use.)
4. Drizzle any remaining sugar mixture over the top of the tree, allowing it to flow down the sides; cool.
5. Remove and discard the cone and foil.

Yield: 12 servings.

Note: You can drop the batter by rounded tablespoonfuls rather than piping it. Recipe makes about 3 dozen pastry puffs.

White Chocolate Mousse with Raspberry Sauce

This dazzling dessert is served in individual white chocolate cups surrounded with a crimson sauce and dotted with whole raspberries.

WHITE CHOCOLATE MOUSSE:

1	envelope unflavored gelatin
1	cup sugar
6	egg yolks
¾	cup cold water
¼	cup Grand Marnier (orange-flavored liqueur)
1	pound high-quality white chocolate, melted
2	cups whipping cream, whipped

WHITE CHOCOLATE CUPS:

3   pounds high-quality white chocolate

Triple recipe of Raspberry Sauce (see recipe in Raspberry and Lemon Cheesecake on page 87)

White chocolate curls and fresh raspberries for garnish

A delicate cup of white chocolate holds a heavenly white chocolate mousse topped with ruby red raspberries.

TO MAKE MOUSSE:

1. In a medium saucepan, combine the unflavored gelatin and sugar. Mix well and set aside.

2. In a medium bowl, whisk together the egg yolks, water, and Grand Marnier until blended. Stir into the gelatin mixture. Cook over medium heat, stirring constantly, until the mixture thickens and a candy thermometer registers 175°. Remove from heat.

3. Gradually whisk in the 1 pound melted chocolate. Pour the custard mixture into a large bowl. Cool 1 hour or until room temperature, stirring often.

4. Stir several large spoonfuls of the whipped cream into the custard mixture. Fold in the remaining whipped cream. Cover and chill.

TO MAKE CUPS:

1. Melt the 3 pounds white chocolate in the top of a double boiler over hot, not simmering, water. Whisk until smooth. Remove from the water bath. Cool to room temperature.

2. Using 12" x 14" pieces of plastic wrap, completely wrap the outside of 8 (8-ounce) plastic foam cups, folding the plastic wrap over the top of the cups and halfway down the inside. Keep the plastic wrap stretched as smoothly as possible.

3. Grasping each cup by its rim, dip the wrapped cups ⅔ of the way into

the melted chocolate. Twirl the cups over the chocolate to let the excess chocolate drip off. Set the dipped cups upright on a tray, keeping them at least 3" apart. Chill until the chocolate is hardened.

4. After 1½ hours, remelt and cool the excess chocolate as in Step 1. Once the chocolate cups have hardened, in about 2 hours, repeat the dipping. Tilt the pan as necessary to make the chocolate deep enough to completely cover the first coat. Chill again for 2 hours. (There will be chocolate leftover. This much is needed to provide enough depth for dipping the cups. Pour the extra chocolate into a storage container; cover and let harden. Use to make chocolate curls for a garnish.)

5. In a cool room with cool hands, work with 1 chocolate cup at a time, keeping the remaining cups chilled. Unfold the plastic wrap from inside the cup. Carefully remove the styrofoam cup by gently squeezing the cup on opposite sides. Continue squeezing around the cup until it releases from the chocolate mold. (You may need to break the foam cup in the process.) Gently peel the plastic wrap from the chocolate cup. Chill while working with the remaining cups.

6. Fill the cups with the white chocolate mousse. Arrange the cups on serving plates. Surround the cups with Raspberry Sauce. Garnish with the white chocolate curls and fresh raspberries.

Yield: 8 servings.

Raspberry and Lemon Cheesecake

Sumptuous wedges of lemony cheesecake are marbleized with a fanciful ribbon of Raspberry Sauce.

GRAHAM CRACKER CRUST:
2 cups graham cracker crumbs
¼ cup sugar
¼ cup unsalted butter, melted
1 egg white

RASPBERRY SAUCE:
2 cups frozen unsweetened raspberries (about 8 ounces)
1 teaspoon lemon juice
½ cup sugar

FILLING:
3 (8-ounce) packages cream cheese, softened
1 cup sugar
Grated zest and juice of 1 lemon
1 cup whipping cream
4 large eggs
Fresh raspberries for garnish

TO MAKE CRUST:

1. In a medium bowl, combine the graham cracker crumbs, ¼ cup sugar, butter, and egg white. Stir until blended. Press in the bottom only of a 9" springform pan. Place the pan on a baking sheet.

2. Bake at 350° for 10 to 12 minutes or until slightly brown. Cool on a wire rack. Reduce oven temperature to 300°.

TO MAKE SAUCE:

1. In a heavy medium saucepan, combine the frozen raspberries, 1 teaspoon lemon juice, and ½ cup sugar. Bring the raspberry mixture to a boil over medium heat, stirring constantly to dissolve the sugar. Remove from heat.

2. Press through a fine sieve to remove the seeds. Cool the sauce.

TO MAKE FILLING:

1. In a large mixer bowl, beat the cream cheese and 1 cup sugar at medium speed of an electric mixer until smooth. Add the lemon zest and juice. Beat well.

2. Gradually beat in the whipping cream at low speed. Add the eggs, 1 at a time, beating at low speed just until blended after each addition. Be careful not to overbeat. Pour the mixture into the prepared crust in the pan.

3. Gently spoon the Raspberry Sauce over the filling in a lacy pattern. Swirl with a toothpick to marbleize.

4. Place a shallow pan of water on the bottom rack of the oven. Place the filled springform pan (without the baking sheet underliner) on the middle rack of the oven directly above the pan of water.

5. Bake at 300° for 2 hours or until almost set in the center. (The cheesecake will still "jiggle" slightly when done.) Cool the cheesecake to room temperature in the pan on a wire rack. Cover and chill thoroughly.

6. Remove the sides of the pan. Garnish the top of the cheesecake with the fresh raspberries.

7. Cut wedges of the cheesecake with a knife that has been dipped in very hot water before each cut.

Yield: one 9" cheesecake.

Trays give a busy hostess an extra pair of hands. Set the tray ahead, and you'll be ready to serve guests when they arrive.

Delightful Details

*Holiday memories are made of little things: a fragrant wreath, handmade gift,
festive touches throughout your home.*

What makes a guest want to linger and eagerly anticipate the next invitation to your home? It's the attention to detail that makes each guest feel welcome and imbues each visit with the spirit of friendship that lasts through the year.

The gestures are simple but telling: Select a single color or combination for your floral arrangements and use it throughout the house as a symbol of hospitality and good cheer.

Seek unexpected places to drape a tiny garland or small swag of fragrant rosemary, thyme, and myrtle: behind a framed photo, around a candleholder, along a chair rail, or at the window seat. Or tuck a sprig of holly and berries into the wine cooler and tie another around the handle of the cake knife.

Set the dessert service on a tray in the living room before dinner and invite guests to join you there

afterwards for coffee and conversation. Display a collection of framed photos of family and friends from holidays past or assemble the pictures in an album on the coffee table. As your guests enjoy sharing your memories, they will become part of them, too.

For a thoughtful favor, prepare a small gift for everyone who shares your holiday: a handmade ornament, homemade sweet, or sachet of seasonal spices or herbs.

An arrangement of red and white roses in a silver trumpet vase picks up the pattern of the damask runner on the sideboard. Red pepper berries are tucked beneath the apricot brandy cake.

A message of peace in the language of flowers, myrtle encircles the base of a silver candlestick.

Organdy ribbon tied at the base holds a pretty hemstitched napkin in a folded fleur-de-lis.

Napkin Folds

Artful arrangement transforms an essential part of the table setting into an extraordinary embellishment.

Any napkin can be folded to suit any occasion: crisp cotton for breakfast or brunch, dainty linen for tea or cocktails, or the finest heirloom damask for a formal dinner.

Tradition calls for a 22"-square napkin at dinner, folded three times to form a rectangle no longer than the diameter of the plate. For a luncheon, an 18" or smaller square should be folded into a triangle pointing away from the plate. But do not let these time-honored rules restrict your creativity; unusual folds signal to your guests that something special is in the air.

The napkin itself can suggest ideas. If it bears an embroidered initial on a corner or delicate tatting along the edge, you may wish to create a fold to highlight the handiwork. Blossoms or greenery used in the centerpiece may be added to the napkin design, perhaps tucked into a luxurious fold or trailing from the cinch of a pleated fan.

Fleur-de-lis Fold

To make this French-accented design, fold the napkin in half diagonally (Diagram 1). Then fold up the bottom folded edge ⅔ toward the top point (Diagrams 1 and 2). Beginning at 1 side of the bottom edge and working toward the other, pleat the napkin (Diagram 3). To secure the pleats, tie them at the bottom of the napkin with a ribbon. Fan the pleats by pulling them out slightly.

There was a row of bouquets all down the table; and on the wide-bordered plates the napkins stood like bishops' mitres, each with an oval-shaped roll between the folds.

— *Gustave Flaubert,* Madame Bovary

Diagram 1

Diagram 2

Diagram 3

A napkin embellished with a crisp bow recalls a gentleman's white-tie ensemble.

Luncheon Fold

This fold is ideal for revealing a corner treatment or monogram on a napkin. To begin, fold the napkin into quarters so the corner design is showing. Place the napkin at an angle, with the free points at the bottom (Diagram 1). Fold down the top corner (Diagram 1). Fold the right corner at a slight angle so it lies slighly past the center of the napkin and then fold the left corner in the same manner (Diagrams 2 and 3). Turn the napkin over to show the corner design or monogram (Diagram 4) and place it on the plate.

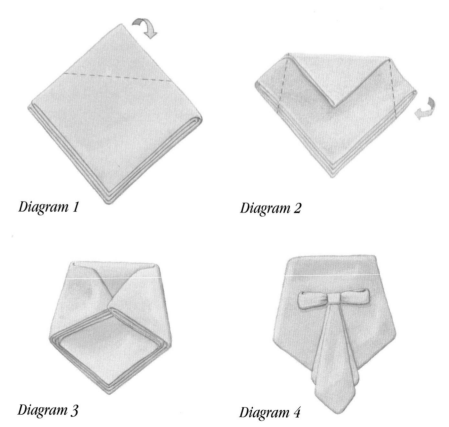

Diagram 1

Diagram 2

Diagram 3

Diagram 4

Column Fold

This simple column shape is especially elegant. Fold the top and bottom edges of the napkin to the center (Diagram 1). Place the napkin on the plate with the seam side down. Then tie the center of the napkin with beautiful cording or ribbon (Diagram 2). Or slip the column through a napkin ring.

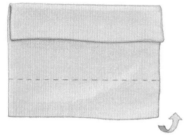

Diagram 1

Diagram 2

Cinched with a length of matching silk cord and a few small blooms, this column shape is especially striking.

Fold History

The art of napkin folding dates to at least the seventeenth century, when writer Guillaume de Rebreviettes marveled at a table setting featuring "napkins disguised as several types of fruit and birds." Before that time, individual napkins—or serviettes, *as the French call them—typically were used at only the finest tables. They often were large enough to cover the entire body and sometimes were shared by two or more diners.*

White-on-white napkins of linen or damask prevailed in Victorian times and were embellished with hemstitching, embroidery, crochet, or tatting. These fine linens were handed down as ceremoniously as heirloom silver, china, and crystal. When properly cared for over the years, the linens appear as pristine and elegant today as when they first graced the table.

Chapter IV

Christmas Dinner

Family and friends gather around a beautifully
set table. The celebration begins
with the Christmas feast.

Christmas Dinner

Traditions are not simply steps we retrace time and again. They are reinvented each year as fresh faces join the family table, bringing new customs and different perspectives. From our menu, select recipes that are sure to become holiday favorites.

MENU

APPETIZERS: Choose one or two.
Warm Spicy Pecans   *Baked Stuffed Mushrooms*
Oysters in Champagne Sauce

BEVERAGES: Choose one or two.
Welsh Nectar   *Citrus Christmas Punch*
Hot Mulled Wine

SOUPS: Choose one.
Apple-Onion Soup   *Lobster Bisque*

ENTRÉES: Choose one or two.
Traditional Roast Pheasant with Fried Breadcrumbs
Marinated Roast Turkey
Baked Ham with Bourbon-Honey Glaze
Minted Lamb Chops in Puff Pastry

SIDE DISHES: Choose two to four.
Cranberry-Almond Conserve   *Fall Fruit Compote*
Cranberry-Apple Relish   *Spiced Apples, Pears, and Prunes*
Pickled Baby Beets   *Brussels Sprout Leaves*
Cornbread-and-Sausage Stuffing   *Maple-Whipped Sweet Potatoes*
Orange-Glazed Carrots

BREADS: Choose one or both.
Roasted Shallot-Caraway Rolls   *Whole Wheat Popovers*

DESSERTS: Choose one or both.
Hot Apricot Fritters with Marzipan Parfaits
Spiced Bread and Apple Pudding

Warm Spicy Pecans

Set a silver bowl of these sweet-hot nuts on the bar. They are a choice complement to cocktails.

BARBECUE SPICE MIX:
2	tablespoons paprika
1	tablespoon chili powder
1	teaspoon sugar
1	teaspoon salt
1	teaspoon ground cumin
1	teaspoon ground coriander
½	teaspoon dry mustard
½	teaspoon black pepper
½	teaspoon dried thyme
½	teaspoon curry powder
¼	teaspoon ground red pepper

SPICY PECANS:
1	cup sugar
4	cups water
4	cups pecan halves

TO MAKE SPICE MIX:
In a small bowl, combine all of the spice mix ingredients; mix well.

TO MAKE SPICY PECANS:
1. Butter a large baking sheet.
2. In a large saucepan, combine the sugar and water. Bring to a boil over high heat, stirring to dissolve the sugar. Add the pecans and cook 5 minutes. Drain the pecans in a colander.
3. Spread the pecans out on a jelly-roll pan. Sprinkle with the spice mix.
4. Bake at 300° for 25 minutes, stirring the pecans occasionally. Serve pecans warm.

Yield: 4 cups.

Baked Stuffed Mushrooms

Garnished for Christmas with fresh cranberries and parsley, these savory bites can be made up to three hours ahead.

2	dozen (about 24 ounces) large fresh mushrooms, about 1½" to 2" in diameter, cleaned
2	tablespoons butter, melted
2	tablespoons olive oil
2	cloves garlic
1	medium onion, cut into eighths
1	pound ground spicy Italian sausage
2	tablespoons fresh breadcrumbs
1	large egg, lightly beaten
2	tablespoons chopped fresh parsley
¾	teaspoon fennel seed
	Dried oregano, basil, and dried crushed red pepper to taste
2	tablespoons freshly grated Parmesan cheese
	Fresh cranberries and fresh parsley sprigs for garnish

1. Cut ends from the mushroom stems. Remove the stems; set aside.
2. Pour the melted butter and olive oil into a 13" x 9" x 2" baking dish. Turn the mushrooms over in the butter and oil mixture to coat and place, cavity up, in the baking dish.
3. Position the knife blade in the food processor bowl; add the garlic and pulse until finely chopped. Add the onion and pulse until finely chopped.
4. In a heavy skillet, sauté the sausage with the garlic and onion until the sausage is done and the onion is tender; break the sausage apart with a spoon as it cooks.
5. In the food processor, chop the mushroom stems. Add to the sausage mixture and cook 2 to 3 minutes. Drain off the fat. Cool the sausage mixture 5 minutes.
6. Add the breadcrumbs, egg, chopped parsley, and fennel seed. Add the oregano, basil, and crushed red pepper to taste.
7. Mound the cooled sausage mixture into the mushroom caps. Sprinkle with the Parmesan cheese. (Mushrooms can be prepared to this point and chilled up to 3 hours.)
8. Bake the mushrooms at 375° for 20 minutes or until sizzling and golden brown. Garnish with the fresh cranberries and parsley sprigs.

Yield: 2 dozen.

The table is a meeting place, a gathering ground, the source of sustenance and nourishment, festivity, safety, and satisfaction.

— *Laurie Colwin*

Oysters in Champagne Sauce

The height of elegance, an appetizer of oysters spells celebration.

CHAMPAGNE SAUCE:
1   tablespoon unsalted butter
2   tablespoons finely chopped shallot
1   cup champagne
1   cup whipping cream
2   tablespoons chopped fresh
      tarragon or 1½ teaspoons dried
      tarragon
½   teaspoon salt
¼   teaspoon pepper

BROILED OYSTERS:
18 fresh oysters on the half shell
2   tablespoons fresh breadcrumbs
Lemon halves
Fresh tarragon sprigs for garnish

TO MAKE SAUCE:
1. Melt the butter in a heavy medium saucepan. Cook the shallot in the butter over medium heat 2 to 3 minutes or until softened.
2. Add the champagne. Boil gently until reduced to ¼ cup. Add the whipping cream and boil gently until reduced by half. Remove from heat.
3. Stir in the chopped tarragon, salt, and pepper. Set aside.

TO MAKE OYSTERS:
1. Arrange the oysters on the half shell on a large jellyroll pan. Lightly coat each oyster with the sauce and sprinkle with the breadcrumbs.
2. Broil 4" or 5" from heat for 4 to 5 minutes or until the oysters are firm and opaque when cut in the center.
3. To serve, arrange 3 oysters on each of 6 serving plates. Cut the lemon halves into a crown or wrap halves in cheesecloth and tie with a ribbon. Garnish with the tarragon sprigs.

Yield: 6 appetizer servings.

Welsh Nectar

Offer this refreshing beverage with brunch or as an alcohol-free choice at cocktail time.

2   lemons
8   ounces sugar cubes, crushed
10   cups boiling water
1⅔   cups raisins, chopped
Carbonated water (optional)

1. Peel the zest from the lemons with a vegetable peeler, avoiding any white pith. Reserve the lemons.
2. In a large bowl, combine the lemon zest and sugar. Pour in the boiling water. Stir until the sugar cubes dissolve. Cover and cool to room temperature.
3. Squeeze the lemons and strain the juice into the zest mixture. Stir in the raisins.
4. Pour into a gallon jar. Close tightly and chill for 4 or 5 days, stirring several times a day.
5. Strain through cheesecloth into clean (sterilized) bottles. Cover and chill. Use within 2 weeks.
6. To serve, pour the nectar into small glasses. Or, if desired, serve in large glasses and add carbonated water to taste.

Yield: 9½ cups.

Citrus Christmas Punch

Plan ahead for this spirited punch— it needs to steep for four weeks.

¼   cup sugar
4   lemons, sliced
2   oranges, sliced
2   teaspoons whole cloves
1½ cups Southern Comfort (sweetened bourbon whiskey)
1½ cups Canadian Club (blended Canadian whiskey)
¾   cup white rum
Boiling water
Cinnamon sticks and lemon twists for garnish

1. In a sterilized 2-quart jar, combine the sugar, lemon slices, orange slices, cloves, sweetened bourbon whiskey, Canadian whiskey, and rum. Mix well, immersing the fruit as much as possible.
2. Seal and chill 4 weeks. Strain through cheesecloth. (Mixture may be cloudy.)
3. To serve, fill heatproof glasses ⅓ full with the liquor mixture. Finish filling the glasses with the boiling water. Garnish with the cinnamon sticks and lemon twists.

Yield: 3½ cups.

Hot Mulled Wine

Warm up carolers or late-arriving guests with a mug of mulled wine flavored with spices of the season.

2 (750 ml) bottles dry red wine
¾ cup port
¾ cup brandy
Zest strips from 1 orange and 1 lemon
1 teaspoon freshly grated nutmeg
6 whole cloves
2 (3") cinnamon sticks
1 tablespoon brown sugar
Orange and lemon zest strips for garnish

1. In a large saucepan, combine the wine, port, brandy, orange and lemon zest strips, nutmeg, cloves, cinnamon sticks, and sugar. Mix well. Bring to a simmer, stirring to dissolve the sugar. Reduce heat and simmer 5 minutes.
2. Strain through cheesecloth.
3. To serve, ladle into heatproof glasses. Garnish with the orange and lemon zest strips.

Yield: about 7 cups.

A Toast to Cinnamon

The aroma of cinnamon signals the senses that it must be the holiday season. Baked goods, winter fruits, and mulled wine invite cinnamon to enhance their flavor.

Cinnamon's source is the dried inner bark of an evergreen, itself a fitting holiday symbol. Left to dry in the sun, the bark rolls into tight curls, which are packaged whole or ground to a fine powder. Most good-quality ground cinnamon is an artful blend of two varieties: the sharper Chinese cinnamon and the milder, sweeter cinnamon of Indonesia. Cinnamon sticks are usually the sturdier Chinese variety, though you may find lighter tan, paper-thin sticks of Indonesian origin in an Asian market.

Dust the tops of baked goods with a mix of ground cinnamon and cocoa or mix ground cinnamon with salt and pepper to season meats such as pork, beef, and lamb before roasting. Top a slice of buttered brioche, raisin bread, or panettone with cinnamon and sugar for cinnamon toast elegant enough to serve with afternoon tea. Add a cinnamon stick to rice pudding, fruit compote, sweet potatoes, pearl onions, dried beans, or stew. Or break the stick into smaller pieces to be added to a marinade for beef or poultry. Impart flavor to coffee, cocoa, or tea by stirring with a cinnamon stick.

*A wreath of fragrant herbs circles hearty **Apple-Onion Soup.***

Apple-Onion Soup

Tart apples and sweet onions get a hearty boost from potatoes in this delectable soup suitable for a first course.

2   (6-ounce) onions, coarsely chopped (3 cups)
2   (8-ounce) potatoes, peeled and cubed (3 cups)
5   (8-ounce) Granny Smith apples, peeled, cored, and cubed (6½ cups)
2   cups peeled, chopped celery root or celery
4   cups chicken stock
2   cups apple cider
Salt and pepper to taste

1. In a large pot, combine the onion, potato, apple, and celery root. Add the chicken stock and cider. Bring to a boil; reduce heat, cover and simmer 40 minutes or until the vegetables are very tender.
2. Puree in a blender in several batches. Return to the pot and reheat over medium heat, stirring often. Season with the salt and pepper to taste. Spoon the soup into serving bowls.

Yield: 10 servings.

Lobster Bisque

A delicacy under any circumstances, lobster reaches new heights of luxury in this creamy soup.

4   quarts water
2   (1½-pound) live lobsters
½   cup vegetable oil
2   stalks celery, diced
1   onion, diced
1   large carrot, diced
1   clove garlic, crushed
½   cup all-purpose flour
3   tablespoons paprika
4   tablespoons tomato puree
1½ teaspoons salt
1   teaspoon pepper
8   cups hot fish stock
3   tablespoons unsalted butter
2   cups half-and-half

1. Bring the 4 quarts water to a boil in a large pot. Plunge the lobsters, head first, into the water; return to a boil. Cover, reduce heat and simmer 10 minutes; drain and cool.

2. Break off the large claws and legs. Crack the claw and leg shells using a seafood or nut cracker. Remove the meat and dice. Set the meat and shells aside.

3. Break off the tails. Remove and discard the stomachs and intestinal veins.

4. Cut the shell of tail segments lengthwise on the underside. Pry open the tail segments. Remove the meat and dice.

5. In a large pot, heat the oil over medium-high heat until hot. Add the celery, onion, carrot, and garlic; cook, stirring constantly, until golden. Add the flour and cook over medium heat 3 minutes, stirring constantly. Add the paprika, tomato puree, salt, and pepper; cook 1 minute, stirring constantly. Add the hot stock and reserved lobster shells. Bring the mixture to a boil, stirring constantly; reduce heat to medium-low and simmer 2 hours, partially covered, skimming occasionally.

6. Strain the stock through a fine sieve into a saucepan. If not serving immediately, dot the surface of the soup with the butter to prevent a skin from forming.

7. Add the half-and-half to the mixture in the saucepan. Bring to a simmer, stirring constantly. Add the reserved lobster meat and simmer, stirring constantly, just until the lobster is heated through.

Yield: 6 servings.

Apples

From brilliant red Rome Beauty to butter-colored Golden Delicious, there's an apple for every eye. Although thousands of varieties are grown around the world, only about 20 are typically available in American markets.

Each variety of apple has different qualities. When choosing apples, consider how they're going to be used. Many varieties listed below are suitable for eating out of hand as well as cooking and baking.

For eating raw, try these varieties of apples that are crisp, juicy, and have a balance of sugar and acid.

Baldwin	Gala	Red Delicious
Empire	McIntosh	Royal Gala
Fuji	Newton Pippin	Spigold

Texture and flavor are the key when choosing apples for cooking and baking. Apples need to be firm and able to hold their shape when exposed to prolonged heat. Use fruit that is at its peak or it will break down too much during baking. These varieties of cooking apples shine when used alone or in combination.

Braeburn	Gravenstein	Russet
Cortland	Jonathan	Stayman
Golden Delicious	Northern Spy	Winesap
Granny Smith	Rome Beauty	York Imperial

Until it's time to use them, let apples share the task of decorating your home for the holidays. Mound an assortment of apples in a pretty bowl and tuck a few sprigs of holly, juniper, or rosemary among them for a stunning centerpiece.

Traditional Roast Pheasant with Fried Breadcrumbs

Roasting the pheasants with bacon moistens and mellows the birds.

ROAST PHEASANT:

3   (2¼) pound whole pheasants (with giblets)
9   slices bacon, halved crosswise
Dried thyme and sage
Chopped fresh parsley
Fresh watercress and fresh lemon thyme sprigs for garnish

FRIED BREADCRUMBS:

4   tablespoons unsalted butter
2   cups fresh white breadcrumbs from firm-textured bread
Salt and pepper to taste
2   tablespoons chopped fresh parsley
Grated zest of 1 orange
4   juniper berries, crushed

TO MAKE PHEASANT:

1. Remove the giblets from the pheasants and reserve for another use. Rinse the birds inside and out with cold water. (Pheasants should now weigh about 2 pounds each.)

2. Place the pheasants on a rack in a shallow roasting pan. Arrange 6 half-slices of bacon, overlapping slightly, across each of the pheasants. Sprinkle generously with the dried thyme and sage.

3. Bake at 425° for 15 minutes. Reduce oven temperature to 400°. Bake 45 to 60 minutes or until a thermometer inserted between the leg and thigh registers 180° and the juices run clear.

4. To serve, arrange the pheasants on a warm serving platter. Sprinkle with the chopped parsley. Garnish with the fresh watercress and lemon thyme sprigs. Serve with the Fried Breadcrumbs.

TO MAKE FRIED BREADCRUMBS:

1. Melt the butter in a medium skillet over medium heat. Stir in the breadcrumbs and salt and pepper to taste. Cook, stirring constantly, or until golden and the texture of coarse sand. Drain well on paper towels.

2. Combine the breadcrumbs, parsley, orange zest, and juniper berries in a serving bowl. Toss to mix.

Yield: 6 servings.

Here is gracious plenty for Christmas dinner: **Traditional Roast Pheasant with Fried Breadcrumbs** *and* **Brussels Sprout Leaves** *(page 112).*

Marinated Roast Turkey

A zesty marinade seasons the turkey with the flavors of hot pepper sauce, mellow shallot, and fresh basil.

MARINADE:
1 cup champagne vinegar
¼ cup water
¼ cup Worcestershire sauce
1 tablespoon lemon juice
½ tablespoon bottled hot pepper
    sauce
¼ cup chopped shallots
¼ cup chopped fresh basil or
    1 tablespoon dried basil
¾ teaspoon salt
¾ teaspoon cracked black pepper
¼ teaspoon ground red pepper
1 cup olive oil
1 cup vegetable oil

ROAST TURKEY:
1 (12-pound) whole turkey

TO MAKE MARINADE:
1. In a large bowl, combine the vinegar and the next 9 ingredients. Whisk until blended.
2. Gradually add the olive oil and vegetable oil in a thin stream, whisking constantly. Set aside.

TO MARINATE TURKEY:
1. Remove the giblets from the turkey and reserve for another use. Rinse the turkey, inside and out, with cold water. Pat dry with paper towels.
2. Arrange the turkey, breast side down, in a large plastic bag set in a shallow roasting pan. (Extra-large oven roasting bags work well.) Whisk the marinade and pour over the turkey. Tie the bag closed, forcing as much marinade as possible up around the turkey.
3. Chill 8 hours or overnight, carefully turning the bag over occasionally.

TO ROAST TURKEY:
1. Remove the turkey from the bag, reserving ½ cup marinade. Arrange the turkey, breast side up, in a shallow roasting pan. Spoon the reserved marinade evenly over the turkey.
2. Roast the turkey at 325° for 3½ to 4 hours or until a meat thermometer inserted in the thickest part of a thigh registers 180°, basting occasionally with the pan drippings.
3. Remove the turkey to a warm platter. Cover the turkey loosely with foil and let stand 15 minutes before carving.
    Yield: 8 to 10 servings.

Baked Ham with Bourbon-Honey Glaze

A sweet bourbon-spiked glaze flavors this boneless ham, which is easy to carve into tender slices.

BAKED HAM:
1 (6-pound) fully cooked whole
    boneless ham
Whole cloves
2 cups apple cider

BOURBON-HONEY GLAZE:
¾ cup firmly packed brown sugar
¼ cup molasses
¼ cup honey
1 tablespoon dry mustard
½ teaspoon ground coriander
2 tablespoons bourbon
2 tablespoons dry sherry

TO MAKE HAM:
1. Trim fat from the ham, if necessary, leaving a layer ¼" thick. Score the fat in a diamond pattern. Stud the center of each diamond with a whole clove.
2. Arrange the ham, fat side up, in a shallow roasting pan. Pour the cider over the ham. Cover the pan tightly with extra-wide heavy-duty aluminum foil, tenting the foil in the

center so it does not touch the top of the ham.

3. Bake at 325° for 2 to 2¼ hours or until a meat thermometer inserted in thickest portion registers 130°, basting with the pan juices every 30 minutes.

TO MAKE GLAZE:

In a small saucepan, while the ham is baking, combine all the glaze ingredients and mix well. Bring the mixture to a simmer over medium heat, stirring to dissolve the sugar. Remove from heat.

TO GLAZE HAM:

1. When the thermometer registers 130°, spoon some of the glaze over the ham.
2. Continue baking, uncovered, for 15 to 30 minutes or until thermometer registers 140°, spooning more glaze over the ham several times.
3. To serve, transfer the ham to a warm platter. Carve into slices.

Yield: 8 to 12 servings.

A Taste of Honey

Honey is a versatile and natural sweetener for beverages, glazes, and dressings. Its subtle variations are as complex as wine, with taste, texture, and color depending entirely on the blossoms favored by its industrious maker, the honeybee. European settlers brought their honeybees to New England in the seventeenth century, using the unrefined results of the bees' industry to make cement, preserve fruit, polish furniture, and cure a variety of aches and pains, as well as to flavor food and drink.

Liquid honey is usually best for cooking, while creme or spun honey is well suited for use as a spread. Honey is sometimes packaged with its edible comb. Many commercial honeys are blended to achieve a consistent taste and color, but honeys made from single pollen sources such as clover or alfalfa are also available. Colors and flavors of honey can vary widely, including

- Alfalfa honey—light and pleasingly mild in flavor
- Basswood honey—white and strong in flavor
- Buckwheat honey—dark and full-bodied in flavor
- Clover honey—usually light amber and mild in flavor
- Eucalyptus honey—variable in color and usually strong in flavor
- Orange blossom honey—light and citrusy in flavor
- Sage honey—light and slightly floral in flavor
- Tulip poplar honey—dark amber and not as strong in flavor as other dark honeys
- Tupelo honey—light, greenish amber, full-bodied but mild in flavor

The more than 300 varieties of honey may be used interchangeably, but if a recipe calls for a specific type that you cannot find, try to match it with a honey of similar color. In general, the lighter the honey, the milder its flavor.

Minted Lamb Chops in a golden puff pastry are accompanied with a silver bowl of Cranberry-Almond Conserve and a bowl of roasted root vegetables.

Minted Lamb Chops in Puff Pastry

Cloaked in golden puff pastry, tender lamb chops benefit from a hint of fresh mint.

12   (3-ounce) rib lamb chops, cut
        1" thick
Salt and pepper
2   (17¼-ounce) packages frozen
        puff pastry sheets (4 sheets)
3   tablespoons chopped fresh mint
1   egg yolk
3   tablespoons water
Cranberry-Almond Conserve (recipe at
        far right)

TO MAKE LAMB CHOPS:

1. Trim off all fat from edge of the lamb chops.
2. Arrange the lamb chops on a rack in a broiler pan. Season with the salt and pepper. Broil 3" to 4" from the heat for 2 minutes.
3. Turn the lamb chops over and broil 2 minutes. Transfer the lamb chops to a baking sheet.
4. Cover and freeze the lamb chops 1 hour.
5. While the lamb chops are in the freezer, thaw the puff pastry according to package directions. On a floured surface, gently unfold 1 sheet of the pastry. Press the pastry together at the 2-fold seam to seal.
6. Roll out the pastry to a 12" square. Cut in 4 (6") squares, trimming the edges evenly. Repeat with 2 more sheets of the pastry, making 12 squares in all.
7. Roll out the last sheet of the pastry and cut out 12 (½" to 1") decorative shapes with small cutters. Wrap and chill pastry.

TO ASSEMBLE:

1. Work with 2 squares of the puff pastry at a time, keeping remaining squares chilled. After lamb chops have been in the freezer 1 hour, remove from the freezer.
2. Position 1 lamb chop in center of each pastry square. Top each lamb chop with ¾ teaspoon mint. Starting at the corners, fold the pastry over the lamb chops, envelope-style, overlapping slightly in the center. (If the rib bones are long, fold the pastry around the bone, leaving the end portion of the bone outside the pastry bundle.) Press the edges of the pastry together to seal.
3. Place the pastry bundles, seam side up, 2" apart on a clean baking sheets. In a small bowl, whisk together the egg yolk and water. Brush over the pastry. Gently press the decorative cutout over the center where dough points come together. Brush with the glaze again.
4. Freeze the pastry for 10 minutes.
5. Bake the pastry bundles at 425° for 15 to 18 minutes or until the pastry is puffed and golden brown. Serve with the Cranberry-Almond Conserve.

Yield: 6 servings.

Cranberry-Almond Conserve

Served here with lamb chops, this fruited mixture is also delicious with pork or poultry.

1   (12-ounce) package fresh or
        frozen cranberries
1   (8-ounce) navel orange, coarsely
        chopped (including peel)
¾   cup sugar
1   cup water
¼   cup slivered almonds, toasted

1. In a large non-aluminum saucepan, combine the cranberries, chopped orange, sugar, and water. Bring to a boil, stirring to dissolve the sugar. Reduce heat to a simmer. Cook until the cranberry skins pop, about 5 to 7 minutes, stirring occasionally.
2. Remove from heat. Stir in the toasted almonds. Serve warm or at room temperature as a relish for lamb, pork, or poultry. Cover and chill any leftover conserve.

Yield: 3½ cups.

Gentle, at home, amid / my friends I'll be /

Like the high leaves / Upon the holly tree.

— *Godey's Lady's Book, 1890*

Spiced Apples, Pears, and Prunes

Baked winter fruits provide a sweet counterpoint for ham, poultry, lamb, or game.

1   cup orange juice
1   cup apple juice
1¼ cups dry white wine
¼   cup firmly packed brown sugar
Grated zest of 1 orange and 1 lemon
2   (3") cinnamon sticks
2   whole cloves
1   (1" piece) fresh gingerroot, finely
       chopped
½   star anise
1   pound cooking apples peeled,
       cored, and cut into sixths
1   pound firm ripe pears, peeled,
       cored, and cut into sixths
¾   cup dried prunes (4 ounces)
Orange zest strips and star anise for
       garnish

1. In a medium bowl, combine the orange juice, apple juice, wine, brown sugar, grated orange and lemon zest, cinnamon sticks, cloves, gingerroot, and ½ star anise. Stir until the sugar dissolves. Set aside.
2. Arrange the apple, pear, and prunes in a deep 3-quart casserole. Pour the wine mixture over the fruit.
3. Cover and bake at 350° for 45 to 55 minutes or until the fruit is almost tender. Uncover and cool.
4. Garnish with the orange zest strips and star anise.
         Yield: 6 servings.

Fall Fruit Compote

Pears and apples marry in a warm compote served with a cherry brandy-spiked custard sauce.

FRUIT COMPOTE:
1   cup cream sherry
1   cup sugar
3   large cooking apples, cored and
       cut into thick wedges
3   large firm ripe pears, cored and
       cut into thick wedges
8   ounces dried figs
8   ounces dried apricots
½   cup currants
1   (3") cinnamon stick

KIRSCH CUSTARD SAUCE:
4   egg yolks
¼   cup sugar
1   cup milk
⅔   cup whipping cream
2   tablespoons kirschwasser
       (cherry brandy)

TO MAKE COMPOTE:
1. In a large pot, combine the sherry and sugar. Bring to a boil, stirring to dissolve the sugar.
2. Add the apple wedges, pear wedges, figs, apricots, currants, and cinnamon stick. Add enough water to cover the fruit. Bring to a simmer. Cover and cook 10 minutes or until the fruit is tender.
3. Remove from heat. Strain, reserving the cooking liquid. Place the fruit in a large bowl; remove and discard the cinnamon stick. Set the fruit mixture aside to cool.
4. Return the cooking liquid to the pot. Boil the cooking liquid until reduced by half. Pour over the fruit. Cool until warm.

5. To serve, spoon the fruit mixture into serving dishes. Ladle the custard sauce over each serving or serve the fruit mixture over pound cake or ice cream.

TO MAKE SAUCE:
1. In a small mixer bowl, beat the egg yolks and sugar at high speed of an electric mixer until thick and pale, about 3 minutes. Set aside.
2. In a medium saucepan, combine the milk and whipping cream. Bring just to a boil. Gradually beat 1 cup of the hot milk mixture into the egg mixture at low speed. Whisk into the remaining hot milk mixture in the saucepan.
3. Cook over medium-low heat, stirring constantly with a wooden spoon, until mixture begins to thicken slightly and coats the spoon. Do not boil. (Mixture will continue to thicken as it cools.) Remove from heat.
4. Strain into a bowl. Stir in the kirschwasser. Press plastic wrap directly on the surface of the custard. Cool to room temperature, about 2 hours.
5. Chill for 4 hours.
         Yield: 8 servings.

Made from apples, pears, currants, and other fruits, **Fall Fruit Compote** *glistens in a cut-glass bowl.*

Relish the Possibilities

A spoonful of chutney, conserve, relish, or jam adds a welcome note of color to the plate as it enlivens a main course or crowns a simple slice of cake. While the difference among these accompaniments can be subtle, you may wish to consider the characteristics of each type when choosing a recipe.

•Chutney *is a fruit or vegetable mixture cooked slowly with sugar, vinegar, and spices, yielding a flavor that grows more mellow with time. Start with fruit that is firm and slightly underripe, so that your chutney will have an agreeably chunky consistency. Brown sugar and malt vinegar will produce a dark rich chutney, but if you prefer a lighter result, use white sugar and white wine vinegar. Chutney improves with age, so allow it to stand at least a month or two before using or giving as gifts. Brush on grilled or roasted meat or poultry (though only at the end of grilling, not before, as the sugar in the chutney will cook quicker than the meat itself) or serve as a condiment with curried dishes, meat, poultry, or fruit and cheese.*

• A conserve *combines two or more fruits cooked with sugar and raisins or nuts. You may serve a conserve as a condiment with the main course, as an ice cream or dessert topping, or as a sandwich spread, perhaps with a slice of turkey or ham.*

• Pickles *and* relishes *are vegetables or fruits pickled with salt and vinegar or preserved with sugar.*

Almost any vegetable or fruit can be pickled, and different combinations of herbs and spices can vary the taste. These savory condiments are best served with meats or vegetables or as a sandwich accompaniment.

• Fruit butter, *such as apple or pear butter, begins with cooked, pureed fruit, which is slowly simmered with sugar and spices until it's thick and creamy and the sugar has caramelized to a pleasing golden color. Apple butter is especially delicious with pork, as well as on biscuits and breakfast breads.*

• Jelly *is made of fruit juices boiled with sugar and pectin and set until firm but still a bit wobbly.* Jam *substitutes crushed or chopped fruit for the juice, making a chunkier mixture.* Marmalade *is a soft, clear citrus jam cooked with the zest and flesh of the fruit.* Preserves *are coarsely chopped fruit or whole fruit, "preserving" the shape of the fruit. Each sweet spread can be used as an accompaniment with rolls, biscuits, muffins, or teacakes; as a filling between cake layers; as a glaze for cheesecake or as a topping for ice cream; instead of maple syrup on waffles; or as a glaze for meat or poultry.*

Follow the recipe exactly for jellies, jams, marmalades, and pickles and preserves and use the best-quality fruit for the finest flavor and color results. If you are a culinary novice, you may find chutney, conserve, and relish recipes easier to master.

Cranberry-Apple Relish

At once sweet and tangy, this relish also boasts the powerful punch of jalapeño pepper.

1   orange
1   Red Delicious apple
1   cup fresh or frozen cranberries
2   teaspoons grated fresh gingerroot
2   teaspoons chopped fresh cilantro
2   teaspoons chopped jalapeño
      pepper
Maple syrup to taste

1. Peel the zest from the orange with a vegetable peeler. Remove the white pith from the orange. Cut the orange pulp in pieces, removing the seeds. Set the pulp and zest aside.
2. Peel and core the apple. Cut into small wedges.
3. Quickly chop the orange zest and pulp, apple, cranberries, gingerroot, cilantro, and jalapeño in a food processor using on/off pulses. Do not puree.
4. Add maple syrup to taste and mix well. Cover and let stand at least 30 minutes before serving. Cover and chill any leftover relish.

Yield: 1⅔ cups.

Pickled Baby Beets

Ruby-hued beets add a lovely touch of color to the Christmas table. Let these baby beets pickle for at least two days before serving.

36 (1-ounce) baby beets or
      3 (16-ounce) cans whole
      small beets, drained
2   cups water
1   cup malt vinegar
¼   cup sugar
1   teaspoon kosher salt
1   sprig fresh thyme
2   teaspoons mixed pickling spice
⅛   teaspoon dried crushed red pepper
1   clove garlic, crushed

1. Trim the fresh beets, leaving ½" of the tops and roots. Place the beets in a Dutch oven; add enough water to cover. Bring to a boil; cover, reduce heat and simmer 15 to 20 minutes or until the beets are almost tender.
2. Drain and cool. Peel the beets, removing the remaining roots and tops. Set aside in a deep large bowl.
3. In a medium saucepan, combine the water, vinegar, sugar, salt, thyme, pickling spice, crushed red pepper, and garlic. Bring to a boil, stirring to dissolve the sugar; reduce heat and simmer 10 minutes. Strain over the beets. Cover and chill at least 48 hours.
4. To serve, spoon the beets into a serving dish, using a slotted spoon.

Yield: 4½ cups.

Orange-Glazed Carrots

Baste baby carrots with honey, brown sugar, orange juice, and lemon.

2   (10-ounce) packages frozen baby
      carrots
½   cup butter or margarine, melted
2   tablespoons brown sugar
1   tablespoon grated orange rind
2   tablespoons fresh orange juice
1   tablespoon honey
2   teaspoons lemon juice

1. Cook the baby carrots according to the package directions until crisp-tender; drain well.
2. Place the baby carrots in an ungreased 1½-quart baking dish. Drizzle the melted butter evenly over the baby carrots. Sprinkle the brown sugar evenly over the baby carrots.
3. Combine the orange rind, fresh orange juice, honey, and lemon juice, stirring well. Drizzle the orange juice mixture over the baby carrot mixture. Bake, uncovered, at 325° for 30 minutes, stirring and basting often.

Yield: 6 servings.

Brussels Sprout Leaves

For this recipe, select medium sprouts that are firm, compact, and bright green in color.

1½ pounds fresh Brussels sprouts
2   tablespoons unsalted butter
1   medium carrot, finely chopped
½   (12-ounce) celery root, finely
    chopped
1   medium onion, finely chopped
2   slices lean bacon, chopped
½   teaspoon dried thyme
1   clove garlic, finely chopped
¼   cup water
½   teaspoon salt
¼   teaspoon pepper
Dash of lemon juice

1. Trim the stem ends of the sprouts. Starting from the stem end, cut out the center core from each sprout with a small knife.

2. Bring a large pot of water to a boil. Add the sprouts and blanch, uncovered, 3 minutes. Remove the sprouts with a slotted spoon and plunge into ice water. Drain. Carefully remove as many of the outer leaves as possible without tearing and set the leaves aside in a colander.

3. Trim the stems from what remains of the whole sprouts and blanch sprouts 3 minutes. Plunge into ice water. Drain and remove most of the remaining leaves. Cut the remaining center portion of each sprout into quarters.

4. Melt the butter in a large heavy skillet over medium-low heat. Add the carrot, celery root, onion, bacon, thyme, and garlic. Cover and cook gently 20 minutes or until soft but not brown, stirring occasionally.

5. Add the water. Bring to a boil over medium-high heat. Add the sprout leaves and quartered centers. Season with the salt and pepper. Stir well. Cook 2 to 3 minutes, tossing constantly, until the leaves are tender but still bright green.

6. Season with the dash of lemon juice.

Yield: 6 servings.

Maple-Whipped Sweet Potatoes

The flavors of apples and maple syrup bring out the best in sweet potatoes.

4   pounds sweet potatoes, cut into
    2" pieces
4   Granny Smith apples, peeled,
    cored, and cut into 2" pieces
2   cups apple cider
½   cup firmly packed light brown
    sugar
2   (3") cinnamon sticks
1   tablespoon ground ginger
2   tablespoons freshly grated nutmeg
Salt to taste
4   tablespoons butter, softened
3   tablespoons lemon juice
½   to 1 cup maple syrup
½   to ¾ cup whipping cream
Salt and ground white pepper to taste

1. In a large saucepan, combine the potato, apple, cider, sugar, cinnamon sticks, ginger, nutmeg, and salt to taste. Add enough water to cover and bring to a boil; cover and simmer 10 to 12 minutes or until tender. Drain the potato, reserving some of the liq-uid. Increase heat to high and reduce the liquid to ½ cup, stirring often.

2. Transfer the mixture to the bowl of a mixer fitted with a paddle attach-ment (or use an electric hand mixer). Beat until smooth. Add the reserved cooking liquid, butter, and lemon juice. Beat until combined. Add the maple syrup, cream, and salt and pepper to taste and beat until well combined.

Yield: 10 to 12 servings.

Cornbread-and-Sausage Stuffing

Aromatic sage, sausage, and celery spark this cornbread stuffing—a favorite in the American South.

5   cups cubed cornbread (about 14
     ounces)
1½ cups toasted fresh breadcrumbs
     from firm-textured bread
3   cups chopped celery
1⅓ cups chopped onion
⅔   cup chopped red bell pepper
½   cup unsalted butter, melted
2   ounces ground pork sausage
1½ tablespoons chopped fresh sage or
     1½ teaspoons dried sage
1   tablespoon chopped fresh parsley
Salt and ground pepper to taste
4   large eggs
½   cup chicken broth

1. Butter an 11" x 7" x 1½" large baking dish; set aside.

2. Combine the cornbread cubes and breadcrumbs in a large bowl. Set aside.

3. In a large skillet, sauté the celery, onion, and red bell pepper in the

butter over medium heat until the vegetables are tender. Pour over the cornbread mixture.

4. Crumble the sausage into the same skillet. Cook over medium heat, stirring often, until browned. Drain. Sprinkle the sausage over the cornbread mixture. Add the sage, parsley, and salt and pepper to taste. Toss to combine. Set aside.

5. In a medium bowl, whisk together the eggs and broth. Pour over the stuffing. Mix gently. Spoon into the baking dish.

6. Bake at 350° for 30 minutes. Cover loosely with foil. Continue baking 15 minutes or until hot and set in the center.

Yield: 8 servings.

Roasted Shallot-Caraway Rolls

Roasting the shallots enhances their subtle sweetness, while toasting the caraway seeds encourages their boldness.

3   (1-ounce) shallots
1½   packages active dry yeast
1   teaspoon sugar
¾   cup warm water (105° to 115°)
1½   cups warm milk (105° to 115°)
2   tablespoons unsalted butter, melted
2   tablespoons honey
5½ to 6 cups bread flour, divided
1   teaspoon salt
1   teaspoon caraway seeds, toasted
1   teaspoon dry mustard
½   teaspoon chili powder

EGG GLAZE:
1   egg beaten with 2 tablespoons water
1   to 2 tablespoons sesame seeds

1. Line a small baking pan with foil. Butter a large bowl. Butter 2 (8" x 8" x 2") baking dishes. Set aside.

2. Place the whole unpeeled shallots in the small baking pan.

3. Bake at 375° for 1 hour. Remove from oven. Cool. Peel and chop the shallots into small pieces. Set aside.

4. Sprinkle the yeast and sugar over the warm water in a small bowl. Stir to dissolve the yeast. Let stand until foamy, about 10 minutes.

5. In a large mixer bowl, combine the milk, butter, honey, and yeast mixture. Beat at medium speed of an electric mixer until blended.

6. Add 2 cups of the flour, salt, caraway seeds, mustard, chili powder, and shallot. Beat at low speed to blend; beat at medium speed 3 minutes.

7. Add 3 cups of the flour, ½ cup at a time, stirring with a wooden spoon until a shaggy dough forms.

8. Turn the dough out onto a lightly floured surface. Knead until smooth and elastic, 5 to 8 minutes, adding enough of the remaining flour 1 tablespoon at a time, as needed.

9. Place in the buttered bowl, turning once to butter the top. Cover with plastic wrap. Let rise in a warm place (85°) until doubled, about 1 hour.

10. Gently punch down the dough. Turn out onto a lightly floured surface. Divide the dough in half.

11. Divide half of the dough into 16 equal portions. Shape each piece into a ball, rolling the edges under to form a smooth top. Gently pinch the dough together at the bottom of each ball.

Arrange the rolls, smooth side up, in one of the prepared baking dishes. Repeat with the remaining dough.

12. Cover the baking dishes loosely with plastic wrap and let rise in warm place until doubled, about 35 to 45 minutes.

13. Brush the rolls with the egg glaze. Sprinkle with the sesame seeds.

14. Bake at 375° for 25 minutes or until golden brown. Remove from the baking dishes. Cool on wire racks just until warm.

Yield: 32 rolls.

Whole Wheat Popovers

Start popovers in a cold oven and serve them immediately, while they are still crisp on the outside and tender inside.

½   cup all-purpose flour
½   cup whole wheat flour
½   teaspoon salt
1   cup milk
3   large eggs, lightly beaten
3   tablespoons vegetable oil

1. Combine all of the ingredients in a mixer bowl; beat at low speed of an electric mixer just until smooth.

2. Spoon the batter into well-greased popover pans, filling ¾ full. Place in a cold oven. Turn oven on 450°; bake 15 minutes. Reduce oven temperature to 350°; bake 30 additional minutes or until crusty and golden. Serve immediately.

Yield: 6 popovers.

Hot Apricot Fritters with Marzipan Parfaits

Think of these as fruit-filled beignets. Serve them nestled next to custard-style parfaits set in a spirited apricot sauce.

MARZIPAN PARFAITS:
4   egg yolks
¾   cup sugar
½   cup boiling water
2   ounces marzipan (also called almond paste; it's found at speciality food stores), cut up
1   cup whipping cream, lightly whipped

APRICOT SAUCE:
1   (6-ounce) package dried apricots
1¼ cups water
2   tablespoons apricot brandy

BATTER:
½   cup milk
2   large eggs
1   cup all-purpose flour
1   teaspoon baking powder
1   teaspoon vegetable oil

APRICOT FRITTERS:
¾   cup water
¼   cup honey
20   dried apricots (about 6 ounces)
1   ounce marzipan, cut up
¼   cup all-purpose flour
Vegetable oil
½   cup superfine sugar

TO MAKE PARFAITS:

1. Lightly butter and sugar 4 (8-ounce) paper drinking cups. Set aside.
2. In a small mixer bowl, beat the egg yolks and ¾ cup sugar at high speed of an electric mixer until thick and pale, about 5 minutes. Beat in ½ cup boiling water at low speed until blended. Pour into top of a double boiler.
3. Cook over simmering water, stirring constantly, until temperature reaches 160°. Remove from the water bath. Stir in the 2 ounces marzipan until melted.
4. Strain into a medium bowl. Press plastic wrap directly on the surface of the custard. Cool to room temperature, about 45 minutes.
5. Remove the plastic wrap. Fold in the whipped cream. Pour into the cups. (Cups will not be full.) Freeze 6 hours or overnight. (Parfaits will not freeze firm.)

TO MAKE SAUCE:

1. In a small saucepan, combine the apricots and enough hot water to cover. Let stand 15 minutes. Drain.
2. Combine the apricots and 1¼ cups water. Bring to a boil; cover, reduce heat and simmer 15 minutes or until tender.
3. Puree the apricots with the cooking liquid and brandy in a blender until smooth. Strain into a bowl. Cool.

TO MAKE BATTER:

In a medium bowl, combine the milk, 2 eggs, 1 cup flour, baking powder, and oil. Beat at medium speed of an electric mixer until smooth. Cover and set aside.

TO MAKE FRITTERS:

1. In a small saucepan, combine the water and honey. Bring to a boil, stirring to dissolve the honey. Stir in the 20 apricots. Cool.
2. Drain the apricots, reserving the syrup for the sauce. Pat the apricots dry on paper towels.
3. Make a small cut in the pit cavity of each apricot and fill with a little piece of marzipan. Dust with the ¼ cup flour.
4. Heat 3" to 4" of oil to 340°. Using 2 bamboo skewers, dip each apricot in the batter, then drop directly into the hot oil. (Do not use frying basket.) Fry 3 or 4 at a time until golden, turning once.
5. Drain on paper towels. Roll in superfine sugar. Serve warm.
6. To serve, gradually stir the reserved syrup into the apricot sauce until blended.
7. Unmold the parfaits onto 4 large serving plates. Alternate 5 fritters and spoonfuls of the apricot sauce around each parfait.

Yield: 4 servings.

Spiced Bread and Apple Pudding

Finish dinner with this exquisite version of classic comfort food.

HONEY SAUCE:
½   cup milk
½   cup half-and-half
4   egg yolks
¼   cup honey
1½ tablespoons Calvados (apple brandy)

CALVADOS SYRUP:
⅓   cup sugar
⅓   cup water
1   tablespoon Calvados (apple brandy)

Fresh raspberries and creamy honey sauce surround a serving of **Spiced Bread and Apple Pudding.**

PUDDING DOUGH:

1 package active dry yeast
¼ cup warm milk (105° to 115°)
Pinch of sugar
1 cup bread flour
1 tablespoon sugar
1 teaspoon pumpkin pie spice
Pinch of salt
1 large egg, beaten
2 tablespoons unsalted butter, softened
2 (7-ounce) Granny Smith apples, peeled, cored, and cut into 12 wedges each
1 tablespoon unsalted butter, melted
1 tablespoon honey
1 tablespoon Calvados (apple brandy)
Fresh raspberries, fresh mint leaves, and confectioners' sugar for garnish

TO MAKE SAUCE:

1. In a small saucepan, bring the ½ cup milk and half-and-half to a boil. Cover and set aside.

2. In a medium bowl, whisk the egg yolks and ¼ cup honey until thoroughly mixed. Gradually add the hot milk mixture, whisking until blended. Pour into a clean saucepan.

3. Cook over medium-low heat, stirring constantly with a wooden spoon, until the sauce thickens and coats the spoon. Do not boil. Strain into a bowl. Press plastic wrap directly on the surface of the sauce.

4. Cool to room temperature, about 2 hours.

5. Cover and chill until cold, about 4 hours or overnight. Remove the plastic wrap. Stir in the 1½ tablespoons Calvados just before serving.

TO MAKE SYRUP:

1. While the sauce is cooling, combine the ⅓ cup sugar and water in a small saucepan. Bring the mixture to a boil. Reduce heat and simmer 5 minutes.

2. Stir in the 1 tablespoon Calvados. Set aside.

TO MAKE PUDDING DOUGH:

1. While the sauce is cooling, sprinkle the yeast over the ¼ cup warm milk and pinch of sugar. Stir until the yeast dissolves.

2. In a medium bowl, combine the flour, 1 tablespoon sugar, pumpkin pie spice, and pinch of salt. Mix well. Add the beaten egg, yeast mixture, and 2 tablespoons butter. Stir with a wooden spoon until blended and a firm dough forms.

3. Cover and let rise in warm place (85°) 30 minutes.

4. While the dough is rising, cook the apple in the 1 tablespoon melted butter in a large skillet over medium heat about 6 minutes or until crisp-tender, stirring often. Drizzle with the 1 tablespoon honey. Stir in the 1 tablespoon Calvados.

TO ASSEMBLE:

1. Butter 4 (1-cup) ramekins. Divide the pudding dough into quarters. Form each quarter into a ball and place in a ramekin.

2. Scatter 6 apple wedges on and around each ball of the dough. Arrange the ramekins on a baking sheet.

3. Cover and let the dough rise in warm place 30 minutes.

4. Uncover and bake at 325° for 25 minutes or until lightly browned. Cool the ramekins on a wire rack 15 minutes.

5. Remove the puddings from the ramekins. Arrange on a wire rack over waxed paper. Spoon the syrup over the puddings several times. Keep warm.

6. To serve, spoon the honey sauce on 4 serving plates. Top with a warm pudding. Garnish with the fresh raspberries, mint leaves, and confectioners' sugar.

Yield: 4 servings.

Chapter V

Holiday Sweets

A treat-laden tea tray, a basket filled with
warm bread, or a generous wedge of pie at the
close of the Christmas feast—proof of
the wisdom of saving the best for last.

Crisp linens cradle **Banana-Pecan Muffins**, *equally welcome at breakfast or teatime.*

Banana-Pecan Muffins

The sweet aroma of this favorite quick bread fresh from the oven will lure a crowd to the kitchen.

3   (5-ounce) very ripe bananas, mashed (1⅓ cups)
1   cup sugar
2   large eggs, lightly beaten
¾   cup canola oil
2   cups all-purpose flour
2   teaspoons baking soda
3   tablespoons buttermilk
1   cup chopped pecans

1. Spray 12 to 14 (2½") muffin cups generously with vegetable cooking spray or line them with paper baking cups.

2. In a large bowl, combine the bananas and sugar; mix well. Add the eggs and oil; stir until blended. Add the flour, baking soda, and buttermilk, mixing well. Stir in the pecans. Fill the muffin cups level full.

3. Bake at 300° for 25 to 30 minutes or until a toothpick inserted in the center comes out clean.

Yield: 12 to 14 muffins.

Braided Anise-Orange Bread

Release the subtle licorice flavor of the anise seeds by crushing them with a rolling pin or mortar and pestle.

1   cup whipping cream or half-and-half
4   tablespoons unsalted butter
⅓   cup sugar
½   teaspoon salt
2   tablespoons anise seeds, crushed
2   tablespoons grated orange zest
1   tablespoon active dry yeast
1   large egg
1   large egg, separated
4   to 5 cups all-purpose flour
2   tablespoons chopped blanched almonds

1. In a saucepan, scald the cream. Remove the pan from heat and add the butter, sugar, salt, anise seed, and orange zest, stirring until the butter is melted.

2. Transfer the cream mixture to a large bowl and let stand until lukewarm. Add the yeast, egg, egg yolk, and 1 cup flour and beat the mixture with a wooden spoon until combined. Stir in the remaining flour, ½ cup at a time, until the mixture forms a dough.

3. Transfer the dough to a lightly floured surface and knead until smooth and elastic, about 5 minutes.

4. Place the dough in a large buttered bowl, turning once to butter the surface. Cover with plastic wrap and a tea towel and let rise in a warm place (85°) until double, about 1½ hours.

5. Punch down the dough. Divide in half. Divide each half into 3 pieces and roll each piece into a rope about 12" to 15" long. Place three ropes side by side on a lightly greased baking sheet and braid. Repeat the procedure with the remaining dough, making sure the loaves are about 2" apart on the baking sheet. Pinch the end of each braid to seal and fold under the loaf.

6. In a small bowl, beat the egg white. Brush the loaves lightly with half of the egg white. Cover with a tea towel and let rise in a warm place for 25 minutes.

7. Brush the loaves with the remaining egg white and sprinkle with the almonds. Bake at 350° for 25 to 30 minutes or until the crust is a deep golden brown and feels firm to the touch and the bottom sounds hollow when tapped.

8. Transfer the loaves to wire racks to cool completely. Serve bread with whipped butter and honey.

Yield: 2 loaves.

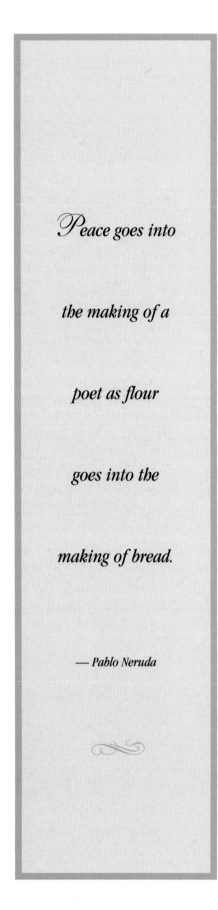

Cinnamon-Swirl Raisin Bread

This recipe yields two loaves: one to share and one for yourself to enjoy. To preserve the shape of the pretty pinwheel filling, let this bread cool completely before slicing through its smooth, golden crust.

DOUGH:

¼	cup warm water (105°to 115°)
	Pinch of sugar
1	package active dry yeast
3	tablespoons sugar
3	tablespoons butter, cut into small pieces
1½	teaspoons salt
2	cups warm milk (105° to 115°)
6½ to 7	cups unbleached all-purpose flour, divided
½	cup dark raisins
½	cup golden raisins

FILLING:

½	cup sugar
1	tablespoon ground cinnamon

TO MAKE DOUGH:

1. Butter 2 (9" x 5" x 3") loaf pans. Butter a 4-quart bowl.

2. Combine the warm water and a pinch of sugar in a small bowl. Sprinkle the yeast over the water mixture. Let stand until the yeast dissolves and bubbles.

3. While the yeast is dissolving, combine the 3 tablespoons sugar, butter, and salt. Pour in warm milk. Stir until the butter almost melts.

4. Stir in 3 cups flour and the dissolved yeast. Beat at high speed of an electric mixer 3 minutes. Stir the raisins into the batter. Stir in enough of the remaining flour with a wooden spoon until the dough forms a ball.

5. Turn the dough out on a well-floured surface. Knead until smooth and elastic, about 8 to 10 minutes, adding enough of the remaining flour to keep the dough from sticking. Place the dough in the buttered bowl, turning once to butter the surface.

6. Cover and let rise in a warm place (85°) until double, about 1¼ to 1½ hours.

7. Punch down the dough. Turn out on a well-floured surface. Divide the dough in half. Cover and let rest 10 minutes.

TO MAKE FILLING:

While the dough rests, combine the ½ cup sugar and cinnamon in a small bowl. Mix well and set aside.

TO ASSEMBLE:

1. Roll half of the dough to a 12" x 8" rectangle. Sprinkle with half of the cinnamon filling. Press the filling into the dough as much as possible.

2. Roll up tightly, jellyroll fashion, starting at the short side. Pinch the dough together at the seam. Pinch the ends to seal and fold under loaf. Arrange seam side down in a loaf pan. Repeat with the remaining dough and filling.

3. Cover and let rise in a warm place until double, about 45 to 60 minutes.

4. Bake at 375° for 45 to 50 minutes tenting loosely with foil during the last 15 minutes of baking time, if necessary, to prevent overbrowning.

5. Remove the pans from the oven. Remove the loaves from the pans. Cool the loaves on wire racks.

Yield: 2 loaves.

Slices of
Cinnamon-Swirl Raisin Bread
*reveal spirals of cinnamon-
and-sugar filling.*

Raisins

It's hard to imagine a handful of dark, crinkly raisins were once a bunch of firm, light green grapes. Ancient Phonecians and Armenians discovered raisins by accident. They found that grapes left too long on the vine had been sun-dried into dark, chewy sweetness. Raisins soon became a prized commodity.

Raisins are still naturally sun-dried and are available in several varieties including muscat, sultana, and golden. You may use them interchangeably in recipes according to your preference. Some recipes suggest "plumping" raisins in hot water or juice to make them softer and less chewy, which may be desirable in a sauce or condiment. In baked goods, toss raisins with flour before stirring into dry ingredients to ensure even distribution.

Currants are smaller, sweeter, sun-dried black Corinth grapes and are not to be confused with the fresh berry with the same name. Dried currants add sweetness to cakes, sweet breads, muffins, and scones.

Gingerbread houses can be simple or elaborate. Twin chimneys and side porches of this marvel take their cues from the painting behind.

Basic Gingerbread House

If you've never baked a gingerbread house, take heart: Even the simplest designs are enchanting.

GINGERBREAD:

1¾ cups sugar
¾ cup honey
4 tablespoons butter or margarine
⅓ cup lemon juice
6 cups all-purpose flour, divided
⅓ cup baking powder
⅛ teaspoon salt
1½ teaspoons ground ginger
1 teaspoon ground cinnamon
1 large egg
1 egg yolk
Gingerbread house pattern on page 138

INEDIBLE ROYAL ICING (see note):
3 egg whites
½ teaspoon cream of tartar
1 (16-ounce) package confectioners' sugar

TO MAKE GINGERBREAD:

1. Combine the sugar, honey, and butter in a large pot; bring to a boil, stirring constantly, until the sugar dissolves. Remove from heat; stir in the lemon juice. Cool.

2. Combine 2 cups of the flour and the baking powder, salt, ginger, and cinnamon in a large mixer bowl. Add the egg, egg yolk, and sugar mixture; beat at medium speed of a heavy-duty electric mixer until blended. Gradually add the remaining 4 cups flour, beating well. Shape into a ball and knead until smooth.

3. Divide the dough in half; wrap 1 portion in plastic wrap and chill. Place the remaining dough on a 16" x 12" greased and floured baking sheet; roll to ⅛" thick, covering the entire baking sheet. Arrange the front, back, and 1 side of the house pattern on the dough. Cut the front, back, and 1 side of the house from the dough; remove the excess dough and chill.

4. Bake cutouts at 325° for 25 to 30 minutes or until firm and golden brown. Remove from the oven. Carefully loosen the gingerbread with a spatula and cool 1 minute on the baking sheet. Transfer to wire racks to cool completely. Repeat the procedure with the remaining dough, cutting the other side of the house and roof pieces. Combine the excess dough and cut the chimney pieces.

TO MAKE ICING:

Beat the egg whites and cream of tartar at high speed of an electric mixer until frothy. Add half of the sugar; beat well. Add the remaining sugar; beat at high speed 5 minutes or until stiff. Icing dries quickly; keep it covered with a damp cloth at all times.

TO ASSEMBLE:

1. Assemble the house, using the Inedible Royal Icing to hold the walls, roof, and chimney together.

2. Decorate the house with the icing.
Yield: one gingerbread house.

Note: For Edible Royal Icing, use meringue powder in place of the egg whites and cream of tartar. Meringue powder is available at kitchen or craft stores. Follow package directions.

Edible Architecture

A gingerbread house can be rustic or elegant, depending on the whim and skill of the baker. Whichever style you choose, planning promises sweet rewards.

• If you want to eat the gingerbread house, keep its size small. Larger houses require sturdier pieces of gingerbread with longer, slower baking times which may make the gingerbread crisper than is desired for eating.

• Pick a sunny day to bake gingerbread. Humidity can cause gingerbread to absorb moisture and soften.

• A large gingerbread house may take two or three batches of dough. If so, make multiple batches rather than doubling or tripling the recipe. If you bake larger pieces of dough than the recipe describes, your baking time may need to increase and baking temperature decrease.

• Cut house pattern templates of lightweight cardboard and use a sharp knife to cut the dough.

• If doors and windows are to be left open or filled with candy "glass," plan to cut out the spaces before baking. To fill windows with candy "glass," crush hard candies (such as Lifesavers) and place in the cutout opening before baking. The candy will melt in the oven and then harden as it cools to form a delicate "stained glass" window.

• To make roof tiles, cut gingerbread rounds with a 1½" cookie cutter; roll the dough quite thin so the shingles will not be too heavy for the walls to support. Or use wafer-thin cookies, round candies, or small squares of shredded wheat for the roof, finishing it with a dusting of confectioners' sugar.

• Assemble the house within 24 hours of baking the gingerbread to keep the gingerbread crisp and firm. If storing the gingerbread overnight, do so in a cardboard box at room temperature.

• For the base of the house, use a large piece of sturdy cardboard or foam board covered with doilies. Cover the bottom with felt or other fabric to prevent scratching the table.

• Pipe icing to outline doors and windows, adding silver dragées for doorknobs and striped gum or wafer cookies for shutters.

• Turn cinnamon sticks, peppermint sticks, or pirolines into porch columns or fence rails. Invert a sugar ice cream cone and frost it to resemble a tree, or plant a fanciful forest of lollipop trees. Create a woodpile from cinnamon sticks or thin pretzels. Marbled rock candy, jelly beans, or nuts can simulate stonework on exterior walls or a path through the snow. Craft a mailbox from a chocolate candy roll perched on a pretzel or cinnamon stick post. Flank the front door with gumdrop topiaries planted in pots made from Lifesavers stacked with icing.

• Small houses made with crisp gingerbread will usually stand a week. Large houses with soft gingerbread may stand only 24 hours.

Pralines

Use only fresh, high-quality nut meats in these candies. Pralines keep best when wrapped in foil and stored in an airtight container.

3   cups sugar
¾   cup milk
½   cup unsalted butter, melted
4   cups pecan pieces

1. In a large saucepan, combine the sugar and milk. Bring the mixture to a boil, stirring constantly, and simmer until it reaches the soft ball stage or until a candy thermometer registers 240°.
2. Remove the pan from heat; add the butter and pecans and stir the mixture until completely combined and slightly thickened.
3. With a tablespoon, arrange the pecan mixture in clumps 1" apart on trays lined with waxed paper. Allow to cool and harden.
4. Store the pralines in an airtight container.

Yield: about 5 dozen.

Brown Sugar Apple Bars

A delicious alternative to brownies, apple bars begin with a sweetly spiced crust of gingersnap crumbs. Finish with a drizzle of creamy custard sauce.

CINNAMON-VANILLA CUSTARD SAUCE:
6   large egg yolks
3   tablespoons sugar
2   cups half-and-half, scalded
1   vanilla bean, split lengthwise
1   (3") cinnamon stick

CRUMB MIXTURE:
1   cup all-purpose flour
1   cup quick-cooking oats
¾   cup gingersnap cookie crumbs
¾   cup firmly packed brown sugar
½   teaspoon salt
½   teaspoon ground cinnamon
¼   teaspoon ground nutmeg
1   cup unsalted butter, cut into small pieces and softened

APPLE FILLING:
¼   cup all-purpose flour
2   tablespoons sugar
2   tablespoons brown sugar
½   teaspoon ground cinnamon
2½ (7-ounce) cooking apples, peeled, cored, and sliced (3 cups)
¼   cup sugar
Fresh strawberries for garnish

TO MAKE SAUCE:
1. In a small mixer bowl, beat the egg yolks and sugar at high speed with an electric mixer until thick enough to form a ribbon when beaters are lifted, about 5 minutes.
2. Slowly beat in the hot half-and-half at low speed. Pour into a large heavy saucepan. Add the vanilla bean and cinnamon stick.
3. Cook over medium-low heat, stirring constantly, until the mixture thickens and coats the back of a spoon. Do not boil.
4. Strain into a bowl. Scrape the vanilla bean seeds into the custard. Discard the cinnamon stick and vanilla bean pod. Press plastic wrap directly on the surface of the custard.
5. Cool to room temperature, about 2 hours. Serve immediately or cover and chill.

TO MAKE CRUMB MIXTURE:
1. Generously butter a 10" x 6" x 1½" baking dish; set aside. In a large bowl, combine the 1 cup flour, oats, gingersnap crumbs, ¾ cup brown sugar, salt, ½ teaspoon cinnamon, and nutmeg; mix well.
2. With a pasty blender or 2 knives, cut in the butter until blended.

TO MAKE FILLING:
1. In a small bowl, combine the ¼ cup flour, 2 tablespoons sugar, 2 tablespoons brown sugar, and ½ teaspoon cinnamon; mix until blended.
2. Pour over the apple in a large bowl and toss to coat.

TO ASSEMBLE:
1. Press ⅔ of the crumb mixture in the bottom of buttered baking dish, reserving the remaining crumb mixture for the topping.
2. Layer the apple mixture mixture evenly over the crust. Top the apple with the remaining crumb mixture and sprinkle with ¼ cup sugar.
3. Bake at 325° for 45 to 50 minutes or until the crumbs are browned and the apple mixture is tender.

4. To serve, cut into bars while warm. Drizzle each serving with custard sauce. Garnish with the fresh strawberries.

Yield: 8 servings.

Rosemary Shortbread Cookies

Cut these buttery treats into simple fluted rounds or another pleasing shape.

1½ cups all-purpose flour
½   cup butter or margarine, chilled
¼   cup sifted confectioners' sugar
2   tablespoons minced fresh rosemary
2   tablespoons sugar

1. Position the knife blade in a food processor bowl; add the first 4 ingredients. Process until the mixture forms a ball.
2. Roll the dough ¼" thick on a lightly floured surface. Cut with a 2" cookie cutter; place on lightly greased cookie sheets.
3. Bake at 325° for 18 to 20 minutes or until the edges are lightly browned. Sprinkle with the 2 tablespoons sugar. Transfer to wire racks to cool completely.

Yield: 1½ dozen.

Rosemary for Remembrance

Rosemary, Shakespeare's symbol of memories, lends its piney fragrance to holiday wreaths and potpourris, and often is clipped into fanciful-shaped topiaries.

But rosemary is more than an ornamental herb. It has long been prized for its curative and culinary properties as well. Rosemary's bold flavor enhances breads, grilled vegetables, roasted potatoes, bean soups, marinades and dry rubs, and is particularly well matched to pork, lamb, and poultry.

Tie sturdy sprigs of the fresh herb into bunches and use as a basting brush or simply toss the bundle onto hot coals to flavor grilled foods. This is one herb that can be substituted in equal amounts whether dried or fresh; whichever you choose, be sure to crush the needles just before using to release their aromatic scent and pungent flavor.

Ginger-Brandy Tea Cake

Baked in a decorative mold and dusted with a snowfall of confectioners' sugar, this aromatic cake is dressed for tea.

CAKE:
½ cup unsalted butter, softened
1 cup sugar
2 large eggs, lightly beaten
½ teaspoon salt
1 teaspoon ground ginger
¼ cup brandy
2 cups unbleached all-purpose
    flour
2½ teaspoons baking powder
½ cup milk
¾ cup chopped crystallized ginger
1 cup coarsely chopped walnuts

GLAZE:
4 tablespoons unsalted butter
¼ cup sugar
¼ cup brandy
Confectioners' sugar

TO MAKE CAKE:
1. Butter a 9" decorative cake mold; dust with flour and shake out the excess.
2. In a large mixer bowl, beat the butter and sugar at medium speed of an electric mixer until light. Gradually add the eggs and beat until well combined. Add the salt, ground ginger, and brandy and beat until combined.
3. Sift the flour and baking powder into a bowl.
4. Add the dry ingredients to the butter mixture alternately with the milk, beating until combined. Fold in the crystallized ginger and nuts.

5. Pour the batter into the mold, and bake at 350° for 50 to 60 minutes or until a cake tester inserted in the center comes out clean.
6. Cool in the mold on a wire rack for 15 minutes and invert the cake onto the wire rack. Poke holes about ¼" deep across the top of the cake with a fork.

TO MAKE GLAZE:
1. In a small saucepan, combine the butter, sugar, and brandy; simmer until slightly thickened. Brush glaze over the cake, repeating until all of the glaze is used.
2. Just before serving, dust with the confectioners' sugar.

Yield: 6 to 8 servings.

Eccles Cakes

Dainty sugar-topped pastries enfold fruit filling spiced with nutmeg. Serve these treats warm or cold with coffee, tea, or a mug of cocoa.

PASTRY:
½ (17¼-ounce) package frozen puff
    pastry sheets (1 sheet)

FRUIT FILLING:
¼ cup currants
1 tablespoon finely chopped candied
    orange or lemon peel
4 teaspoons packed brown sugar
⅛ teaspoon ground nutmeg
⅛ teaspoon ground allspice
1 teaspoon unsalted butter,
    softened
1 large egg, lightly beaten
Sugar

TO MAKE PASTRY:
Thaw the pastry sheet at room temperature 20 to 30 minutes.

TO MAKE FILLING:
1. While the pastry is thawing, combine the currants, candied peel, brown sugar, nutmeg, and allspice; mix well.
2. Add the butter and stir until blended.

TO ASSEMBLE:
1. Gently unfold the pastry sheet onto a floured surface. Cut the pastry into 3 long strips along seam lines.
2. Roll out each strip to a 13" x 5" rectangle. Using a 2" cutter, cut 12 circles out of each pastry strip, making 36 in all.
3. Spoon ½ teaspoon fruit filling in center of each pastry circle. Brush the edges of pastry with the beaten egg. Fold in all 4 sides of the pastry over filling, envelope-fashion, pinching the edges together to seal.
4. Turn the filled pastries seam side down. Roll gently with a rolling pin just until the currants are visible under the pastry. Arrange, seam side down, 1" apart on a baking sheet. Prick a hole in the center of each pastry with a meat fork. Sprinkle the pastries with the sugar.
5. Cover with plastic wrap and let stand 20 minutes. Uncover the pastries.
6. Bake to 375° for 15 minutes until golden. Remove from oven and serve warm or cold.

Yield: 3 dozen.

Fruit-filled **Eccles Cakes** *lavish a silver tray along with miniature mince pies and shortbread wedges.*

Petits Fours

A classic teatime treat, these pretty little cakes are iced to resemble tiny presents. The gift inside? Ganache.

CAKE:
½   cup unsalted butter, softened
¾   cup sugar
2   large eggs, lightly beaten
½   cup sour cream
1   teaspoon vanilla extract
½   teaspoon almond extract
1½ cups all-purpose flour
¾   teaspoon baking powder
¼   teaspoon salt

GANACHE:
6   ounces bittersweet chocolate
¾   cup whipping cream

MARZIPAN COATING:
1   pound marzipan (also called almond paste; it's found at specialty food stores)
2   to 3 cups confectioners' sugar
Liquid food coloring

TO MAKE CAKE:
1. In a mixer bowl, beat the butter and sugar at medium speed of an electric mixer. Gradually add the beaten eggs, sour cream, and flavorings, beating until blended.
2. Sift the flour, baking powder, and salt into a bowl. Add the dry ingredients to the butter mixture and beat until combined.
3. Pour the batter into a buttered and floured 9" springform pan and bake at 350° for 45 to 60 minutes or until a cake tester inserted in the center comes out clean.

4. Transfer the cake to a wire rack to cool for 5 minutes. Invert onto the rack to cool completely. Chill the cake until very cold.

TO MAKE GANACHE:
1. Position the knife blade in the food processor bowl; add the chocolate and process until chopped.
2. In a small saucepan, bring the cream to a simmer. With the processor running, add the cream to the chocolate until the chocolate is melted and smooth. Transfer the mixture to a bowl; cover and chill until firm enough to spread.

TO ASSEMBLE:
1. Split the cake and fill with the ganache. Cut the cake into small squares.
2. In a mixer bowl, beat the marzipan and enough confectioners' sugar at medium speed of an electric mixer to form a pliable and not too sticky dough. (Set aside about ¼ of the marzipan for the ribbons, if desired.) Add the 2 or 3 drops of food coloring to the remaining marzipan and beat until well blended. Add additional confectioners' sugar as needed.
3. Transfer the marzipan coating to a clean counter and using confectioners' sugar as flour, roll to ⅛" thick. Cut the marzipan into squares larger than the cake squares. Place a marzipan square over each cake square and smooth down the edges.
4. Add 2 or 3 drops of contrasting food coloring to the reserved marzipan and beat until the marzipan is well blended. Add additional confectioners' sugar as needed. With the contrasting color of marzipan, make

strips to resemble ribbons and secure with a little water atop cake square to look like presents.
    Yield: about 2 dozen.

Rolled Quince Cobbler with Spiced Syrup

Traditional cobbler is reinvented here, made in jellyroll fashion for a spectacular presentation.

SPICED SYRUP:
2   cups sugar
1   cup water
1   cup apple cider
¼   teaspoon ground cinnamon
¼   teaspoon ground nutmeg

BISCUIT DOUGH:
2   cups all-purpose flour
2   teaspoons baking powder
1   teaspoon salt
½   teaspoon baking soda
½   teaspoon sugar
⅓   cup unsalted butter, cut into small pieces
¾   cup plus 2 tablespoons buttermilk

FILLING:
1   tablespoon unsalted butter, melted
2   cups peeled, chopped quince or Golden Delicious apple
Confectioners' sugar

TO MAKE SYRUP:
1. In a medium saucepan, combine the syrup ingredients; mix well. Bring to a boil, stirring to dissolve the sugar.

2. Reduce heat. Boil gently until the mixture is reduced to 2¼ cups. Remove from heat and cover to keep warm.

TO MAKE DOUGH:

1. Butter a 13" x 9" x 2" baking dish; set aside.

2. In a large bowl, combine the flour, baking powder, salt, baking soda, and ½ teaspoon sugar; mix well. Cut in the ⅓ cup butter with a pastry blender until the mixture resembles coarse meal.

3. Make a well in the center of the dry ingredients. Add the buttermilk, stirring just until the dough pulls away from the sides of the bowl.

4. Turn out onto a well-floured surface. Knead gently with fingertips 10 times or until smooth. Roll out to a 12" x 9" rectangle.

TO MAKE FILLING:

1. Brush the dough with the melted butter. Sprinkle the chopped quince on the dough, leaving a 1" border on all sides.

2. Roll up, jellyroll-fashion, starting with long side. Fold ends under. Pinch ends and bottom seam to seal.

TO ASSEMBLE:

1. Arrange the roll, seam side down, in the center of the baking dish. Carefully pour 1 cup syrup around the roll, reserving the remaining syrup.

2. Bake at 350° for 45 to 50 minutes until the roll is lightly browned and the dough is done. (Watch the roll carefully so the syrup does not burn.)

3. Remove from the oven. Immediately use slotted spatulas to lift the roll onto a serving platter. Cool the roll 20 minutes.

4. To serve, dust the roll with the confectioners' sugar. Cut the warm roll into thick slices and serve with reserved syrup.

 Yield: 8 servings.

Jelly Tartlets

If you are the lucky recipient of a gift of basil or currant jelly, here is an elegant use for it. Bake tiny tarts with a creamy cheese filling, then top them with a spoonful of the not-too-sweet jelly.

PASTRY:
2	cups all-purpose flour
½	teaspoon salt
½	cup unsalted butter, cut into small pieces
3	tablespoons shortening
4	to 5 tablespoons ice water

CREAM FILLING:
1	(8-ounce) package cream cheese, softened
2	tablespoons milk

TOPPING:
Purple basil jelly or current jelly

TO MAKE PASTRY:

1. Position the knife blade in the food processor bowl; add the flour and salt. Add the butter and shortening. Pulse until the mixture resembles coarse meal.

2. With the processor running, gradually add the ice water, processing until the dough pulls away from the sides of bowl and forms a ball. Divide the dough in half. Form each half into a disk shape.

3. Wrap and chill 30 minutes.

TO MAKE FILLING:

In a small mixer bowl, combine the cream cheese and milk. Beat at medium speed of an electric mixer until fluffy.

TO ASSEMBLE:

1. Spray 32 (1¾") miniature muffin cups with vegetable cooking spray.

2. Roll out half of the dough on a floured surface. Cut the dough in 16 (2½") rounds. Reroll the pastry as necessary. Fit the pastry into the muffin cups. Repeat the procedure with the remaining half of the pastry.

3. Spoon about ½ tablespoon of the filling into each pastry cup. Arrange the muffin tins on baking sheets.

4. Bake at 400° for 25 minutes or until the crust is nicely browned. Remove from the pans. Cool on wire racks.

5. To serve, spoon the jelly atop each cooled tart.

 Yield: 32 tartlets.

Christmas Puddings

Prepare your puddings on the Sunday before Advent, a tradition known as "Stir-up Sunday." Store the puddings in the refrigerator and reheat them in a steam bath as directed below.

1   cup self-rising flour
1   teaspoon pumpkin pie spice
1   teaspoon ground cinnamon
¼   teaspoon ground nutmeg
5   cups fresh white breadcrumbs from firm-textured bread
1⅓   cups firmly packed brown sugar
1   cup unsalted butter, chilled and cut into 1" pieces
3   cups currants
1⅓   cups golden raisins
1⅓   cups dark raisins
⅔   cup chopped candied orange or lemon peel
½   cup slivered almonds
2   tablespoons molasses
Grated zest and juice of 1 lemon
2   tablespoons rum or brandy
3   large eggs
1¼   cups brown ale or stout
¼   cup brandy, warmed

1. Butter 2 deep 6-cup heatproof bowls. Set racks in the bottom of 2 deep pots large enough to hold a 6-cup bowl. Fill the pots with water to a depth of 2" to 3". Bring the water to a boil while making the puddings.

2. In a large bowl, combine the flour, pumpkin pie spice, cinnamon, and nutmeg; mix well. Stir in the breadcrumbs and brown sugar until blended. With a pastry blender or 2 knives, cut in the butter until the mixture resembles coarse crumbs.

3. Add the currants, golden and dark raisins, candied peel, and almonds to the bowl; mix well and set aside.

4. In a small saucepan, cook the molasses over medium-low heat, stirring constantly, until warm. Remove from heat. Stir in the lemon zest, juice, and 2 tablespoons rum. Add the eggs, whisking until blended. Stir into the fruit mixture; mix well. Gradually add the ale, stirring until blended.

5. Divide the batter between the buttered bowls. Cover with a double thickness of waxed paper, then foil. Tie tightly with string around rim of the bowls. Trim off the long ends of the paper and foil.

6. Using oven mitts, place the bowls on racks in pots of boiling water. The water should come halfway up sides of the bowls. Bring the water to a boil; reduce heat.

7. Cover the pots and boil gently 6 to 7 hours or until a toothpick inserted in the center comes out clean, adding more boiling water as necessary during steaming.

8. Carefully remove the bowls from the pots. Uncover the bowls and cool the puddings in bowls set on wire racks 1 hour. Carefully loosen the edges of the puddings with a knife. Unmold onto serving platters. Cool until warm, about 45 minutes.

9. To serve, pour the warm brandy into a ladle. Ignite. Carefully pour over the warm puddings. Cut into wedges.

Yield: 2 puddings
(6 to 8 servings each.)

Note: Puddings may be cooled completely, wrapped in plastic wrap, then foil and stored in the refrigerator up to 2 months. Reheat puddings in a buttered bowl in a steam bath, as directed, about 2 hours or until warmed through before serving.

To ovensteam puddings: Set the racks on the bottom of large deep pots. Pour in hot water to a depth of 1". Prepare the puddings as directed. Place the covered pudding bowls in pots. Cover the pots. Bake at 325° for 4 hours or until a toothpick inserted in the center comes out clean. Continue following directions beginning with Step 8.

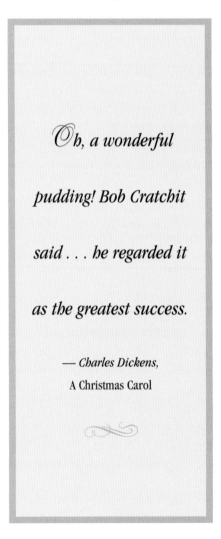

Oh, a wonderful pudding! Bob Cratchit said . . . he regarded it as the greatest success.

— Charles Dickens,
A Christmas Carol

Old-Fashioned Piecrust Dough

A blend of sweet butter and shortening produces a perfectly flaky crust. Use it to make any of the three pies that follow.

2½   cups unbleached all-purpose flour
1   tablespoon sugar
1   teaspoon salt
½   cup unsalted butter, chilled and cut into 1" pieces
½   cup shortening, cut into 1" pieces
1   large egg
¼   cup ice water

1. In a large bowl, whisk together the flour, sugar, and salt. With a pastry blender or 2 knives, cut in the butter and shortening until the mixture resembles coarse meal. Set aside.
2. In a small bowl, whisk together the egg and ice water. Gradually pour into the flour mixture, stirring with a fork until the dough begins to cling but does not form a ball.
3. Turn the dough out onto a lightly floured surface. Lightly work the dough with the heel of hand or fingertips until the dough forms a ball.
4. Wrap in plastic wrap and chill at least 2 hours or overnight.
Yield: pastry for one 9" double-crust pie or two 9" pastry shells.

Peach-Raspberry Pie

The rich lattice crust is even prettier when you cut the strips with a fluted pastry wheel.

PEACH-RASPBERRY FILLING:
¾   cup sugar
2   tablespoons plus 1 teaspoon instant tapioca
½   teaspoon ground cinnamon
1½   pounds fresh peaches
1½   teaspoons fresh lemon juice
2   cups (10 ounces) fresh or frozen unsweetened red raspberries

EGG GLAZE:
1   large egg
3   tablespoons cold water

PASTRY:
Old-Fashioned Piecrust Dough (recipe at left)
Sugar
Vanilla ice cream

TO MAKE FILLING:
1. In a small bowl, whisk together the ¾ cup sugar, tapioca, and cinnamon. Set aside.
2. Peel, halve, and pit the peaches. Cut each half into 4 slices. Measure 3½ cups into a large bowl. Add the lemon juice, sugar mixture, and raspberries. Mix gently.
3. Let stand 15 minutes.

TO MAKE GLAZE:
In a small bowl, beat together the egg and water. Set aside.

TO MAKE PASTRY:
1. On a lightly floured surface, roll out ⅔ of the pastry. Fit into a 9" pie plate.
2. For the lattice top, roll out the remaining pastry to a 13" diameter circle. Cut into 8 (1½"-wide) strips. Brush the strips with the egg glaze and sprinkle with a little sugar.

TO ASSEMBLE:
1. Pour the filling into the pastry shell. Arrange the lattice strips over the filling in a crisscross pattern.
2. Trim the bottom crust edge and lattice strips to a 1" overhang. Fold the bottom crust edge over the lattice strips to form a thick edge; flute the edge with thumb and forefinger. Place the pie plate on a baking sheet.
3. Bake at 425° for 40 to 45 minutes or until the pastry is browned and the juices are bubbling. Cool on a wire rack.
4. Serve with vanilla ice cream.
Yield: one 9" pie.

Golden Apple Pie

A glistening top crust hints of the buttery sweetness within. Golden Delicious apples hold up beautifully during baking and slicing.

APPLE FILLING:
3   pounds large Golden Delicious apples
1½ tablespoons fresh lemon juice
¼   cup sugar
¼   cup firmly packed brown sugar
2   tablespoons cornstarch
¾   teaspoon ground cinnamon
⅛   teaspoon ground nutmeg

EGG GLAZE:
1   large egg
3   tablespoons cold water

PASTRY:
Old-Fashioned Piecrust Dough (recipe on page 131)
2   tablespoons unsalted butter, softened
Sugar
Vanilla ice cream

TO MAKE FILLING:
1. Peel, core, and quarter the apples. Cut each quarter into 3 wedges. Measure 8 cups of the apple wedges into a large bowl. Toss the apple wedges with lemon juice. Set aside.
2. In a small bowl, whisk together the ¼ cup sugar, brown sugar, cornstarch, cinnamon, and nutmeg. Sprinkle over the apple. Mix gently until evenly coated.

TO MAKE GLAZE:
In a small bowl, beat together the egg and water. Set aside.

TO MAKE PASTRY:
1. On a lightly floured surface, roll out ½ of the pastry. Fit into a 9" pie plate.
2. Roll out the remaining pastry to a 12" diameter circle.

TO ASSEMBLE:
1. Mound the apple filling in the pastry shell. Using both hands, press and shape the filling to form a tightly packed, high mound. Trim the bottom crust to ½" overhang, reserving the pastry scraps. Dot the filling with the butter.
2. Arrange the top crust over the filling, patting the crust gently with hands so the pastry conforms to the shape of the filling. Trim the top crust to 1" overhang, reserving the pastry scraps. Fold the top crust under edge of the bottom crust. Flute the edge, pressing together with the thumb and forefinger.
3. Reroll the pastry scraps to make 3 large diamond-shaped leaves, each about 2½" long. Use the tip of a knife to draw lines to simulate leaf veins. Brush the backs of leaves lightly with egg glaze, then arrange leaves in center of the pie, bending slightly to give a natural look. Reserve the remaining egg glaze.
4. Cut 5 or 6 vents around the center of top crust for steam to escape. Place the pie on a baking sheet.
5. Bake at 425° for 20 minutes.
6. Reduce oven temperature to 375°. Bake an additional 30 minutes.
7. Brush the top of the pie with the remaining egg glaze and sprinkle with sugar. Bake 10 minutes or until the pastry is golden brown and the juices are bubbling in center. Cool on a wire rack.
8. Serve slightly warm with vanilla ice cream.

Yield: one 9" pie.

Lemon Meringue Pie

To maintain its elegant shape, spread the meringue all the way to the edge of the filling and seal to the pastry before baking.

PASTRY:
½   recipe Old-Fashioned Piecrust Dough (recipe on page 131)

LEMON FILLING:
1   cup sugar
6   tablespoons cornstarch
¼   teaspoon salt
1¾ cups cold water
4   egg yolks
2   teaspoons grated lemon zest
½   cup fresh lemon juice
3   tablespoons unsalted butter, cut into small pieces

MERINGUE:
4   egg whites
¼   teaspoon cream of tartar
Pinch of salt
½   cup superfine sugar
¾   teaspoon vanilla extract

TO MAKE PASTRY:
1. On a lightly floured surface, roll out the pastry. Fit into a 9" pie plate. Trim and flute the edge. Prick the pastry shell all over with the tines of a fork.
2. Line the pastry shell with foil and fill with dried beans. Place the pie plate on a baking sheet.

3. Bake at 425° for 15 minutes. Remove the beans and foil.

4. Bake the pastry shell an additional 5 to 10 minutes or until it is lightly browned. Cool on a wire rack.

TO MAKE FILLING:

1. In a heavy non-aluminum medium saucepan, combine the sugar, cornstarch, and ¼ teaspoon salt. Whisk until the mixture is blended and no lumps remain.

2. Whisk in the cold water until the mixture is smooth. Bring to a boil over medium heat, stirring constantly. Boil and stir 1 minute. Remove from heat.

3. In a medium bowl, whisk the egg yolks, gradually adding the hot sugar mixture.

4. Bring to a boil over medium heat, stirring constantly. Cook and stir 2 minutes. Remove from heat.

5. Stir in the lemon zest, lemon juice, and butter, stirring until the butter melts. Pour into the cooled pastry shell. Cool slightly while preparing the meringue.

TO MAKE MERINGUE:

1. In a large mixer bowl, beat the egg whites, cream of tartar, and salt at low speed of an electric mixer until the mixture is foamy. Beat at high speed until soft peaks form.

2. Gradually beat in the superfine sugar, 1 tablespoon at a time, beating until stiff, glossy peaks form, scraping the sides of bowl often. Beat in the vanilla.

TO ASSEMBLE:

1. Using a large spoon, pile the meringue on top of the filling, mounding higher in the center and spreading out to the edges of the pastry. Seal the meringue to the edge of pastry. Use the back of a spoon to create swirls in the meringue. Place the pie plate on a baking sheet.

2. Bake at 325° for 25 to 28 minutes or until the top is golden brown. Cool on a wire rack 4 hours before serving. (Pie is best eaten the same day it is baked.)

3. Cover and chill any leftover pie.

Yield: one 9" pie.

Classic Coconut Cake

The crowning glory of the Christmas feast: a triple-layer cake adorned with fluffy white frosting and a cloud of coconut.

CAKE:
1½ cups sugar
1 cup vegetable oil
3 large eggs
2 cups all-purpose flour
2 teaspoons baking powder
½ teaspoon baking soda
½ teaspoon salt
1 cup buttermilk

FILLING:
½ cup butter or margarine
1 cup sugar
1 cup evaporated milk
3 egg yolks
1 teaspoon vanilla extract
1½ cups flaked coconut

FROSTING:
1 cup light corn syrup
½ cup sugar
3 egg whites
½ cup flaked coconut

TO MAKE CAKE:
1. In a large mixer bowl, beat the 1½ cups sugar and oil at medium speed of an electric mixer until blended. Add the 3 eggs, 1 at a time, beating after each addition.
2. Combine the flour, baking powder, soda, and salt; add to the sugar mixture alternately with the buttermilk, beginning and ending with the flour mixture. Mix at low speed after each addition until blended. Pour the batter into 3 greased and floured 8" round cake pans.

3. Bake at 350° for 20 to 25 minutes or until a toothpick inserted in the center comes out clean. Cool in the pans on wire racks 10 minutes; remove from the pans and let cool completely on the wire racks. Cover and set aside.

TO MAKE FILLING:
1. Melt the butter in a small heavy saucepan; add the 1 cup sugar, milk, and 3 egg yolks. Cook over medium heat, stirring constantly, until the mixture thickens and comes to a boil. Boil 1 minute, stirring constantly. Remove from heat; add the vanilla and stir well. Cool completely.
2. Stir in the 1½ cups coconut. Spread the coconut mixture between the cake layers. Set aside.

TO MAKE FROSTING:
1. Combine the syrup and ½ cup sugar in a small heavy saucepan. Cook over medium heat, stirring constantly, until clear. Cook, without stirring, until a candy thermometer registers 232°.
2. While the syrup cooks, beat the 3 egg whites until soft peaks form; continue to beat, adding the hot syrup in a heavy stream. Continue beating just until stiff peaks form and the frosting is thick enough to spread.

TO ASSEMBLE:
1. Immediately spread the frosting on the top and sides of cake.
2. Sprinkle the ½ cup flaked coconut on the top of the cake. Cover and chill thoroughly.
    Yield: one 3-layer cake.

Fruit-Filled Walnut Cake Roll

The key to success when making a cake roll is to move swiftly. Roll the cake while it's warm and allow it to cool before filling and rerolling.

CAKE ROLL:
⅔ cup all-purpose flour
1 teaspoon baking powder
¼ teaspoon salt
3 large eggs
¾ cup sugar
⅓ cup water
1 teaspoon vanilla extract
⅓ cup ground walnuts
2 to 3 tablespoons confectioners' sugar
1 cup whipping cream
½ teaspoon ground cinnamon
1 teaspoon vanilla extract
Coarsely chopped walnuts and apple slices for garnish

CRANBERRY-APPLE FILLING:
2 large cooking apples, peeled, cored, and chopped
1 cup fresh cranberries
¼ cup sugar
¼ cup water
2 tablespoons brandy
1 teaspoon lemon juice
½ teaspoon ground cinnamon
¼ teaspoon ground nutmeg

TO MAKE CAKE ROLL:
1. Grease a 15" x 10" x 1" jellyroll pan. Line the bottom of the pan with waxed paper; grease waxed paper. Set aside.
2. Combine the flour, baking powder, and salt; set aside. In a large mixer bowl, beat the eggs at high speed of an electric mixer 2 minutes. Gradually add the sugar, beating 5

minutes or until thick and pale. Stir in the water and 1 teaspoon vanilla. Gradually fold the flour mixture and ground walnuts into the egg mixture with a wire whisk. Spread the batter evenly in the prepared pan.

3. Bake at 375° for 12 minutes or until the cake springs back when lightly touched in the center.

4. Sift the confectioners' sugar in a 15" x 10" rectangle on a cloth towel. When the cake is done, immediately loosen from the sides of the pan and turn out onto the towel. Peel off the waxed paper. Starting at the narrow end, roll up the cake and towel together; place, seam side down, on a wire rack to cool.

TO MAKE FILLING:
Combine all the filling ingredients in a medium saucepan. Cook over medium heat, stirring constantly, about 10 minutes or until the cranberry skins pop and mixture is thickened. Let cool completely.

TO ASSEMBLE:
1. Unroll the cake; spread with the cranberry mixture. Reroll the cake without the towel; place, seam side down, on a serving plate.

2. Beat the whipping cream, ½ teaspoon ground cinnamon, and 1 teaspoon vanilla at high speed until stiff peaks form. Spread the whipped cream mixture over the cake or spoon the mixture into a decorating bag fitted with a metal tip and pipe over the cake. Garnish with the walnuts and apple slices.
    Yield: one filled cake roll
        (5 to 6 servings).

Cranberries

Some families still brighten the branches of their Christmas trees with traditional strings of fresh cranberries. And few would consider their holiday meal complete without the accompaniment of the sweet-tart taste of cranberry relish or jelly.

One of only three fruits native to North America (the others are blueberries and Concord grapes), cranberries boast a color made for Christmas. The journey from bog to bag includes a stop at the sorting station, where low-quality berries are culled and good ones are still put to a nineteenth-century test: the bounce. Each cranberry is given several chances to bounce over a four-inch wooden wall. Bruised or overripe fruit will not bounce, while cranberries with the proper firmness will agreeably hop across.

Fresh cranberries make their debut in the marketplace in the fall and will keep fresh for months in the freezer. When using frozen berries, do not thaw, but use them straight from the freezer. To prepare for cooking, sort berries, remove all stems, and rinse in cold water. Cook cranberries only until they begin to pop; otherwise, their tartness will turn unpleasantly bitter.

Stir chopped fresh cranberries and orange zest into apple pie filling or grind raw cranberries with apples, oranges, and sugar or honey for a delightful holiday relish.

*H*oney Curd Cake with Orange Flower Water *is baked in a sweet pastry shell, set in a pool of orange sauce and crowned with confectioners' sugar.*

Honey Curd Cakes with Orange Flower Water

Immensely popular in nineteenth-century England and often used in French and Middle Eastern cooking, orange flower water is a fragrant distillation of fresh orange blossoms. Purchase it in small quantities, for it loses its potency over time.

SWEET PASTRY:
2⅔ cups all-purpose flour
3 tablespoons superfine sugar
13 tablespoons unsalted butter, cut
    into small pieces
Finely grated zest from 1 lemon
2 egg yolks, lightly beaten

ORANGE SAUCE:
4 tablespoons arrowroot
1½ tablespoons orange juice
3 tablespoons superfine sugar
1⅔ cups orange juice
1 teaspoon orange flower water

HONEY CURD FILLING:
4 teaspoons cornstarch
1 tablespoon water
1½ teaspoons orange flower water
3 egg yolks
1 cup cream-style cottage
    cheese
⅔ cup whipping cream
2½ tablespoons honey
1 egg white, stiffly beaten
Confectioners' sugar
Caramelized orange zest strips and
    fresh mint sprigs for garnish

TO MAKE PASTRY:
1. In a medium bowl, combine the flour and 3 tablespoons superfine sugar. Add the butter. Knead with hands until the mixture starts to cling together.
2. Add the lemon zest and 2 lightly beaten egg yolks. Knead until the dough forms a ball.
3. Divide the dough in half. Shape each half into a disk. Wrap in plastic wrap and chill 30 minutes.

TO MAKE SAUCE:
1. While the pastry is chilling, combine the arrowroot and 1½ tablespoons orange juice in a small bowl, stirring until smooth. Set aside.
2. In a small saucepan, combine the 3 tablespoons superfine sugar, 1⅔

cups orange juice, and 1 teaspoon orange flower water. Cook over medium heat, stirring constantly, until the sugar dissolves.

3. Stir in the arrowroot mixture. Cook, stirring constantly, until thickened. Do not boil. Strain into a bowl. Press plastic wrap directly on the surface of the sauce. Cool to room temperature.

TO MAKE FILLING:

1. In a small bowl, stir together the cornstarch, water, and 1½ teaspoons orange flower water until smooth. Set aside.

2. In a medium bowl, whisk the 3 egg yolks. Stir in the cottage cheese, whipping cream, honey, and cornstarch mixture. Mix well. Fold in the beaten egg white.

TO ASSEMBLE:

1. Cut each dough disk in quarters. On a lightly floured surface, roll out each pastry quarter to a 5" round. Fit the pastry rounds into 4" tartlet pans. Trim edges.

2. Set the pans on a baking sheet. Ladle the filling evenly into the pastry shells.

3. Bake at 350° for 30 minutes until the filling is set and golden brown.

4. Cool in the pans on a wire rack 15 minutes. Remove from the pans. Cool on a wire rack.

5. To serve, arrange the orange curd cakes on 8 serving plates. Dust with the confectioners' sugar. Garnish with the caramelized orange zest strips and mint sprigs. Spoon the orange sauce around the cakes.

Yield: 8 servings.

Persimmon Ice Cream

Choose only perfectly ripe persimmons, those with a deep orange color and green cap attached, to assure a sweet, spicy flavor.

5	extra-large egg yolks
½	cup plus 1 tablespoon sugar, divided
1	cup whipping cream
¾	cup milk
2	or 3 persimmons, peeled, pitted, and chopped
1	teaspoon lemon juice

1. In a small mixer bowl, beat the egg yolks and ½ cup sugar at high speed with an electric mixer until thick and pale, about 5 minutes. Set aside.

2. Combine the whipping cream and milk in a small saucepan. Bring to a boil over medium heat. Immediately remove from heat. Cool slightly. Gradually beat into the yolk mixture at low speed.

3. Strain through cheesecloth or an extra-fine sieve into the top of a double boiler. Cook over simmering water, whisking constantly, until a thermometer registers 160°.

4. Pour into a medium bowl. Press plastic wrap directly on the surface of the custard. Chill until cold, about 4 hours.

5. Puree the persimmons with the lemon juice and remaining 1 tablespoon sugar in a blender. Measure 1 cup. Strain into the cold custard and mix well.

6. Pour into an ice cream machine. Freeze according to manufacturer's directions.

7. Cover and freeze 4 to 6 hours.

Yield: about 1 quart.

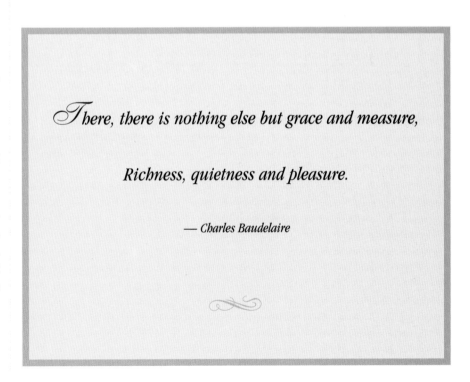

There, there is nothing else but grace and measure,

Richness, quietness and pleasure.

— *Charles Baudelaire*

Basic Gingerbread House Pattern

Recipe and instructions are on page 122.

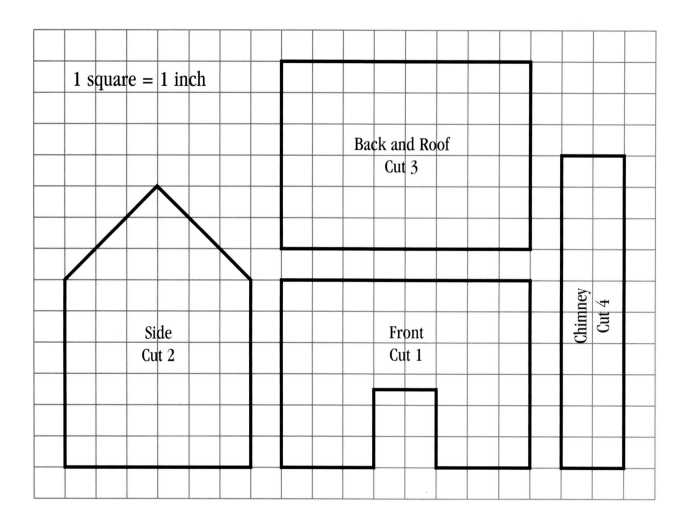

1 square = 1 inch

Back and Roof
Cut 3

Side
Cut 2

Front
Cut 1

Chimney
Cut 4

Stitch Instructions

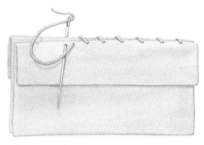

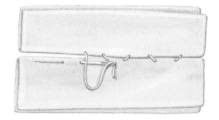

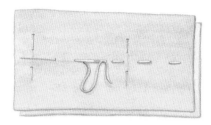

Whipstitch
Use this stitch to sew together two finished edges or to attach a trim to an edge. With the right sides facing, stitch over the edges, keeping the stitches even and close together.

Slipstitch
Use this almost invisible stitch to attach a finished edge to a flat piece of fabric. To make the stitch, slip the needle under the fold in the fabric.

Basting stitch
Use this stitch to temporarily mark seams and patterns on fabric or to temporarily hold fabric pieces together. Remove basting stitches after sewing work is finished.

Woven-Ribbon Ornament Pattern

Instructions are on pages 40–41. Pattern includes ½" seam allowance.

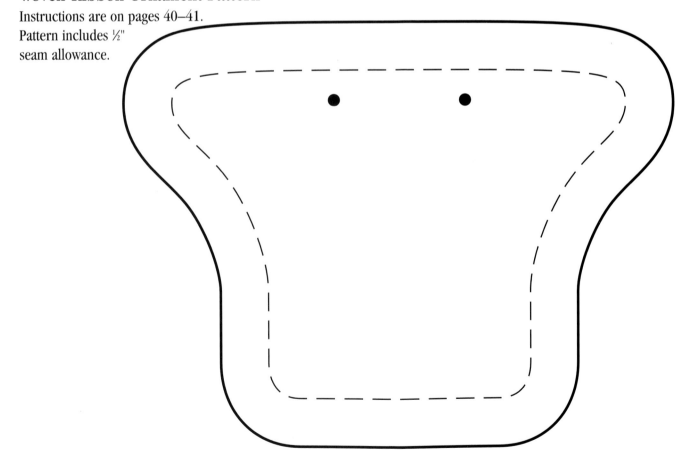

CRAFT FOAM AND FLORIST'S FOAM:
Schrock's International
P.O. Box 538
Bolivar, OH 44612
(330) 874-3700

DECORATIVE RUBBER STAMPS:
Hot Potatoes
2805 Columbine Place
Nashville, TN 37204
(615) 269-8002 (catalog $5)

ESSENTIAL OILS:
Essential Oil Company
1719 Southeast Umatilla Street
Portland, OR 97202
(800) 729-5912

EVERGREEN TREES, GARLANDS, AND WREATHS:
Laurel Springs Christmas Tree Farm
7491 Highway 18 South
P.O. Box 85
Laurel Springs, NC 28644
(800) 851-2345

FABRIC:
Schumacher
79 Madison Avenue
New York, NY 10016
(800) 332-3384

HANDBLOWN GLASS ORNAMENTS:
Old World Christmas
P.O. Box 8000
Spokane, WA 99203
(800) 962-7669

HANDMADE PAPERS:
Loose Ends
P.O. Box 20310
Keizer, OR 97307
(503) 390-7457

HERBS AND DRIED NATURALS:
Tom Thumb Workshops
14100 Lankford Highway
Route 13
P.O. Box 357
Mappsville, VA 23407
(757) 824-3507

HOLLY:
Green Valley Growers
10450 Cherry Ridge Road
Sebastopol, CA 95472
(707) 823-5583

RIBBON:
Midori, Inc.
3524 West Government Way
Seattle, WA 98199
(206) 282-3595.

Offray Ribbon Company
360 Route 24
Chester, NJ 07930
(908) 879-4700

WAX SEALS AND WAX:
Victorian Papers
P.O. Box 411341
Kansas City, MO 64141
(800) 718-2380

WIRE-MESH CONES:
SNK Enterprises
P.O. Box 6702
Chesterfield, MO 63006
(314) 991-8570

Recipe and Designer Credits

Café Bon Homme
Plymouth, Michigan
White Chocolate Mousse with Raspberry Sauce, page 86
Raspberry and Lemon Cheesecake, page 87

Doblin
Fabric on cover

Flowering Design
Wreath and garland, cover
Greenery, page 18

Gore Hotel
London, England
Traditional Roast Pheasant with Fried Breadcrumbs, page 102
Brussels Sprout Leaves, page 112
Spiced Apples, Pears, and Prunes, page 108

Lauren Groveman
Cinnamon-Swirl Raisin Bread, page 120

Holly Henderson
The Lavender Heart
Pages 45, 62 (bottom)

Margot Hotchkiss
Page 41

Hurd Orchards
Holley, New York
Apple-Onion Soup, page 100

Marsha Hyll
Spongeware Farm
Pages 28–29, 30 (bottom)

Little Pie Company
New York, NY
Lemon Meringue Pie, pages 132–133

Locke-Ober Restaurant
Boston, Massachusetts
Lobster Bisque, pages 100–101

Lygon Arms
Worcestershire, England
Spiced Bread and Apple Pudding, pages 114–115
Honey Curd Cakes with Orange Flower Water, pages 136–137

Rita Morrison
Pages 56–59

Camela Nitschke
Page 40

Nan Norseen
Misty Meadows
Page 6

Old World Christmas
Pages 32–35

Mary Benagh O'Neil
Hot Potatoes
Pages 52–55

Dondra Parham
Pages 64–67, 74–77

Catherine B. Pewitt
Pages 36, 38 (left), 72–73

Trisha Romance
Page 122

Lisa Santarelli
Fiori
Page 2

Schumacher
Pages 46–47

Emelie Tolley
Pages 18–19

Raymond Waites
Page 24

Sally Waldrup
Page 38(right), 39

Patricia G. Weaver
Pages 48–51, 60–61

Ron Wendt
Pages 42–43, 44

Cynthia M. Wheeler
Pages 52–53, 68–71

Wickwood Country Inn
Saugatuck, Michigan
Banana-Pecan Muffins, page 119

Windsor Court Hotel
New Orleans, Louisiana
Eccles Cakes, page 126

Photography Credits

Photographers:

Jim Bathie
Back of cover (top right and
bottom right), pages 16, 20, 21, 22–23,
36, 38, 39, 41, 48–49, 50–51, 53, 54,
56, 59, 60, 61, 62 (top), 63, 64, 65, 69,
70,71, 72, 75, 77

Pierre Chanteau
Pages 81, 106, 109

Steve Cohen
Pages 102–103

Christopher Drake
Pages 115, 136

Tom Eckerle
Pages 90, 92, 93

Katrina De Leon
Page 133

Gross & Daley
Pages 7, 28, 29, 30 (bottom)

Jim Hedrich
Pages 13 (top), 84, 86, 118

Brit Huckabay
Cover fabric, pages 10–11 (border), 37,
46–47 (border), 66, 78–79 (border), 94–95
(border), 116–117 (border)

Michael Jensen
Back of cover (left), page 5

Tina Mucci
Pages 46–47, 96, 121

Starr Ockenga
Pages 6, 12

Toshi Otsuki
Cover, pages 2, 9, 14–15, 17, 18, 19,
24, 25, 31, 32, 34–35, 89 (right),
94–95, 122

Luciana Pampalone
Pages 26, 27, 40

Steven Randazzo
Pages 30 (top), 116–117

Michael Skott
Pages 45, 62 (bottom)

William P. Steele
Pages 3, 10–11, 13 (bottom), 42–43,
44, 78–79, 82, 88, 89 (left), 100, 127

Photo Stylists:

Mary Baltz
Pages 42–43, 44

Roscoe Betsill
Food styling, pages 81, 106, 109

Rebecca Borden
Food styling, pages 102–103

Kay Clarke
Back of cover (top right and
bottom right), pages 16, 20, 21, 22–23,
36, 38, 39, 41, 48–49, 50–51, 53, 54,
56, 59, 60, 61, 62 (top), 63, 64, 65, 69,
70,71, 72, 75, 77

Nicole Esposito
Back of cover (top right and
bottom right), pages 16, 20, 21, 22–23,
36, 38, 39, 41, 48–49, 50–51, 53, 54,
56, 59, 60, 61, 62 (top), 63, 64, 65, 69,
70,71, 72, 75, 77

Vinny Lee
Pages 115, 136

Acknowledgments

At Hearst Communications, Inc.:

Kim Bealle

Gina Frank

David Graff

Fran Reilly

Risa Turken

Bridges Antiques
Birmingham, AL

Christine's
Birmingham, AL

Henhouse Antiques
Birmingham, AL

Lamb's Ears, Ltd.
Birmingham, AL

Carolyn and John Hartmann

Index